Haynes for HOME DIY

HOME SECURITY

The complete guide to a safe and secure home and family

Sonia Aarons and Donna Gilbert
Edited by Derek Jones

First published in 1994
2nd Edition 1995

© Sonia Aarons and Donna Gilbert 1995

Published by:
Haynes Publishing
Sparkford, Nr Yeovil, Somerset BA22 7JJ

British Library Cataloguing-in-Publication Data:

A catalogue record for this book is available from the British Library.

ISBN 1 85960 100 6

Printed in Great Britain by J H Haynes & Co Ltd.

**While every effort is taken to ensure the accuracy of the
information given in this book, no liability can be accepted by
the author or publishers for any loss, damage or injury
caused by errors in, or omissions from, the information given.**

Foreword

Fighting crime is something we can all do, and is something we must all do. As Director of Community Action Trust which set up the Crimestoppers initiative in 1988 I heartily welcome a book which helps us all make life more difficult for the criminal.

Practical crime prevention measures such as those described in this book are essential. It is equally important that those who commit crimes are detected and brought to justice and Crimestoppers, now a nationwide scheme, has been extremely successful in encouraging us all to report information and suspicious activity which may eventually lead to an arrest and a conviction.

This initiative has also contributed to an increase in crimes that have been cleared up and has helped to recover millions of pounds worth of property.

Crime is a widespread problem, affecting everybody, young and old, working and retired, and requires a concerted effort by society to tackle it. While levels of home security protection have increased since 1988, it is alarming that in a fifth of incidents entry doors or windows have been left open or unlocked.

It is vital we take a stand and in order to fight crime, fight apathy too. 'If it doesn't affect me, it doesn't concern me' is too often the state of mind. Yet one day it may. If you see what you believe to be a crime taking place, report it to the police. If a Crimestoppers poster or campaign jogs your memory, all you need to do is pick up the phone and dial 01800 555111. You don't even need to give your name. And if your call leads to an arrest and charge you may receive a cash reward.

Home Security is playing its part in helping to improve awareness of what can be done, very often quite simply and cheaply, to increase our effectiveness in preventing crime and making it an easier task for our hard-pressed police to catch the criminal.

Initiatives such as Crimestoppers are just one way you can help the police. Reading *Home Security* and making practical use of its wide range of useful advice, is another.

Digby Carter
Director, Community Action Trust

Contents

Chapter 3   87

Outdoor Security

Chapter 4   101

Personal Security

Chapter 5   117

Vehicle Security

Chapter 6   133

Crime and its prevention

Essential information   144

Introduction

This book tackles Home Security in six ways –

- **Securing the Home** – choosing and fitting locks, bars, grilles and glazing for doors and windows.
- **Indoor Security** – dealing with topics such as checking visitors, fitting alarms, security marking, safes and insurance.
- **Outdoor Security** – including external lights, common-sense precautions outside the house and precautions while you're away from home.
- **Personal Security** – including advising children, helping the elderly and sensible precautions while travelling.
- **Vehicle Security** – covering crime prevention for cars, caravans, bikes and boats.
- **Crime and its prevention** – examining crime, its causes and prevention, local crime-prevention groups, and sources of further information.

Spot the victim...

Take two houses at night. One is in darkness, the other has lights on and a hi-fi can be heard. Or two houses during the day. One has windows open, a dog in the garden and a radio playing indoors. The other appears to be completely shut up - the windows are closed, except for a small fanlight round the side, the house is silent and there's milk on the door step.

Which house would you burgle?

These simple instances show how important it is to make your house look occupied as well as to make it secure. Eight out of ten burglaries occur when the house is empty, often because the owners have failed to take adequate security measures.

Then find the way in...

Once a burglar believes that a house is unoccupied, he will study what security measures you have taken. Even if you have fitted locks to windows and doors do you use them every time you leave the house, even for a few seconds?

In three burglaries out of ten, an intruder gets in through a door or window that has been carelessly left open. Seventy per cent of burglaries involve forced entry, but this may mean no more than lifting poorly-secured patio doors from their tracks, levering a back door with a jemmy, or forcing a window secured with a traditional fastener.

There are many reasons for deciding to improve the security of your home - you've been burgled yourself or there have been break-ins in the area; or a Neighbourhood Watch scheme has alerted you to the importance of home security; or you've just

moved into a new house or you want to qualify for home contents insurance discounts.

To start, it helps to know where your home is most vulnerable. Sixty-four per cent of burglars break in through the rear of a property; 28 per cent through the front; 6 per cent through the side and 2 per cent through the roof. So, if you are working on a tight budget, it pays to prioritise and secure areas according to their vulnerability.

Nobody is immune

The type of home you live in also needs to be considered. Contrary to popular belief, burglars do not concentrate only on expensive detached houses or suburban semis. Council flats and houses are just as much at risk.

A terraced house may back on to neighbouring properties, so the front will be more vulnerable. An upper-storey flat may only provide access via a front door, so your efforts should be concentrated here. Detached houses offer most opportunities as there is often easy access to the side and rear, so all vulnerable entry points will have to be properly secured.

Bungalows may offer access via all windows and possibly skylights. People living in remote areas may need an intruder alarm linked to a central monitoring station. If the house isn't visible to neighbours or passers-by, a burglar will have more time to overcome physical security devices. A remotely-monitored alarm will ensure that his entrance to your home is detected, and the emergency services alerted immediately.

Security survey

To help you to identify the weak links in your security and take the appropriate action, complete the simple security check at the end of this section. But first, you will need to carry out a survey of your home. You can do this yourself (ideally with a friend for a more objective appraisal) or, if you prefer, contact the Crime Prevention Officer at your local police station, who will be happy to take a look at your property and advise you accordingly.

Lock up, as you would do when you were going out, then stand outside the property and pretend you have lost your keys. How easy would it be to gain access? Obviously you'll want to cause as little damage as possible, but you will probably spot at least three or four points for easy entry, and you will be doing what thieves do during their pre-call investigation.

These points of entry normally include the back door, front door and ground floor windows, and are gained by breaking a small area of glass, using brute force or even by reaching through the letter box for the door key hanging on a string. Alternatively, a small fanlight left open upstairs could be reached by the ladder laying in the back garden. If your back door is still fitted with the traditional 2-lever lock – the 'builders' lock' – a burglar may have a key that fits or be able to pick the lock with a piece of wire.

Once you have improved security, it's important to remember to use it – even if you're only popping down the road for a few minutes – and combine it with common-sense measures to avoid letting your home look unoccupied.

Is this you?

Notes left on the door inform unwelcome passers-by of your absence.

Where to start and what it costs

Once you realise you need to improve the security of your home, knowing where to start is crucial. Basically, prevention measures can be split into three categories - common-sense precautions, physical security and electronic security.

Physical security covers locking mechanisms such as door and window locks and padlocks, door chains and viewers, security marking, security doors, grilles and shutters and safes. Electronic security covers intruder alarm systems, security lighting, audio and video door entry systems, and closed circuit television monitoring.

When protecting your home, always give priority to physical security, fitting good locks to all exterior doors and accessible windows. This is the first step in any home security campaign.

Obviously the level of security will depend on your available budget, so concentrate on the basics. It's no good spending £150 on a safe if you haven't secured your home against entry in the first place. About 50 per cent of burglars break in through windows and 48 per cent through front, rear or side doors, so it's sensible to concentrate your efforts on these areas. If you fit the locks, you can achieve a good level of physical security for under £100 for an average semi-detached property. This figure is based on five lever mortise deadlocks fitted to the front and rear doors, a door chain, door viewer and locks fitted to eight windows.

If you can invest a larger sum, consider securing outbuildings with locks or padlocks and installing security lighting devices. If you have a lot of valuables to protect, or live in a high risk area, consider fitting an intruder alarm system. A professionally installed system may set you back £400 or more, but a DIY system will cost nearer £150. The initial outlay may seem expensive but it's a small price to pay for the security of your home and family. And check with your insurance company - by fitting the right products you could qualify for discounted rates on your home contents insurance.

If you feel you need to consult more experienced people or professional associations before undertaking your DIY security project, turn to the chapter on 'Getting Advice' in Chapter 6, where we list some of the many trade associations and professional bodies which are reliable sources of information.

Check your security rating

Convinced your home is secure? Get together with your family and spend a few minutes answering each question – honestly – to find out whether your security is really up to scratch.

Just tick the appropriate letter next to each question, then see what your final score reveals.

YOUR HOME AND ITS CONTENTS

		Always or Yes	Usually	Sometimes	Never
1	If you were uncertain about the security of your home, would you seek advice from the police, a locksmith, or other security expert?	A	B	C	D
2	Are all your exterior doors fitted with security deadlocks?	A	B	C	D
3	Is the back door also secured with mortise bolts and/or hinge bolts (or, if it is UPVC, a multi-point locking system)?	A	B	C	D
4	If you have a patio door, is it fitted with locks, top and bottom?	A	B	C	D
5	Are all easily accessible windows fitted with security locks?	A	B	C	D
6	Do you always lock doors and close and lock windows when going out?	A	B	C	D
7	Do you always keep your door keys in a safe place (i.e., not attached to a piece of string that can be pulled through the letter box, or under the door mat)?	A	B	C	D
8	Do you keep exterior doors locked when there is nobody in the house and you are out in the garden or garage?	A	B	C	D
9	Do you own either a dog that barks or an intruder alarm system?	A	B	C	D
10	Have you installed a smoke detector in your home?	A	B	C	D
11	Is your front door fitted with a door chain or limiter?	A	B	C	D
12	Is your front door fitted with a spy hole, video door entry system, or glass nearby which enables you to view callers?	A	B	C	D
13	Do you always put the door chain on before opening the door?	A	B	C	D
14	Do you thoroughly check the identity of strangers at the door before letting them in?	A	B	C	D
15	If you were suspicious about any travelling salesmen or callers, would you report them to the police or a Neighbourhood Watch co-ordinator?	A	B	C	D
16	Do you belong to a Neighbourhood Watch scheme?	A	B	C	D
17	Do you have a Neighbourhood Watch sticker displayed in your window?	A	B	C	D
18	Do you keep video recorders and other valuables out of sight of passers-by?	A	B	C	D
19	Have you postcoded or security-coded your property?	A	B	C	D
20	Have you displayed a sticker in your window informing passers-by that the property is security marked?	A	B	C	D
21	Have you photographed smaller items of value which cannot be postcoded?	A	B	C	D
22	Have you made a list of your property, including serial numbers and distinguishing features?	A	B	C	D
23	Do you avoid keeping large sums of money in the house?	A	B	C	D

YOUR HOME AND ITS CONTENTS *(continued)*

		Always or Yes	Usually	Sometimes	Never
24	Are you adequately insured?	A	B	C	D
25	Can you say that you have never left a note taped to the door for delivery men, stating that you are out?	A	B	C	D
26	Do you always collect your milk from the doorstep and your post from the letter box promptly?	A	B	C	D
27	Do you avoid leaving the curtains drawn by day?	A	B	C	D
28	When you go out, do you ever leave a radio playing?	A	B	C	D
29	Do you leave lights on when you go out after dark?	A	B	C	D
30	Are any of your lights fitted to timeswitches?	A	B	C	D
31	When you go on holiday, do you inform neighbours or the police?	A	B	C	D
32	Do you ask a neighbour or friend to pop in and collect the post and generally keep an eye on the place?	A	B	C	D
33	When you are going away, do you always cancel the milk and papers?	A	B	C	D

AROUND AND ABOUT

		Always or Yes	Usually	Sometimes	Never
34	Is your front door visible to passers-by?	A	B	C	D
35	Is your home overlooked?	A	B	C	D
36	Are ladders locked away, or secured firmly to a wall?	A	B	C	D
37	Are you certain that bricks and rubble are not available in your garden?	A	B	C	D
38	Do you always lock garden tools away?	A	B	C	D
39	Is it difficult to gain access to the side or rear of your property?	A	B	C	D
40	Are side passages or back gates secure?	A	B	C	D
41	Do you close and lock the garage when you go out?	A	B	C	D
42	Do you lock the garage at night?	A	B	C	D
43	Is your garden shed secured with a padlock or other locking device?	A	B	C	D
44	If yes, do you always remember to use it?	A	B	C	D
45	Have you installed lights around your home?	A	B	C	D
46	Is the streetlighting in your area adequate, and in working order?	A	B	C	D
47	If you didn't feel that streetlighting was adequate, would you mention it to the police or local authority?	A	B	C	D
48	If you saw a stranger loitering in your area, and acting suspiciously, would you report it to the police?	A	B	C	D
49	Do you have the telephone number of your local police station to hand?	A	B	C	D
50	Are you confident that you have taken all reasonable steps to beat the burglar?	A	B	C	D

Turn over to work out your final score

Now add up your score

Add up the number of As, Bs, Cs and Ds and write the total of each in the table ▶. Then award yourselves:
6 points for every **A**; **4** points for every **B**; **2** points for every **C** and **0** points for every **D**, and enter the totals in the table ▶.

If you scored:
225-300: Congratulations. You've obviously given a great deal of thought to the security of your home. Your score indicates that your physical security is up to scratch and you remember to take common-sense precautions to beat the burglar. Be careful to remain vigilant and not become complacent.

150-224: You've obviously thought about the security of your home, but there's still room for improvement. Take another look at your physical security to see if it can be improved, and remember to put all these common-sense measures into practice when you leave home, or answer the door to strangers.

75-149: Definitely room for improvement here. There are plenty more steps you can take to improve security. Put some of the suggestions included in our checklist into action, and if you are concerned about the security of your home contact the Crime Prevention Officer at your local police station for some free advice.

0-74: It's all too easy to think 'it won't happen to me', but with statistics for burglary and theft continuing to rise you cannot afford to be complacent. Take advice NOW to improve security and check your security rating again in a few months' time.

Number	
A	x 6 =
B	x 4 =
C	x 2 =
D	x 0 =
FINAL SCORE =	

Principal points of entry

Front door	**25**%
Rear/side door	**23**%
Rear/side window	**43**%
Front window	**3**%
Upper window	**3**%

Main methods of entry

Forced door or window . .	**40**%
Insecure door or window .	**22**%
Break glass	**21**%
Use a key	**3**%
Other	**3**%

Burglaries: the facts

1 One dwelling is burgled every 50 seconds.

2 Eight out of ten burglaries occur when the house is empty.

3 Seventy per cent of burglaries involve forced entry.

4 In three burglaries out of ten, a door or window has been left open.

5 Two-thirds of burglaries are carried out during the week.

6 The peak age for offenders is 15.

7 Most burglaries are opportunistic and 80 per cent of burglaries are not committed by professionals.

8 Only one in eight homes has adequate security locks.

An Open Invitation

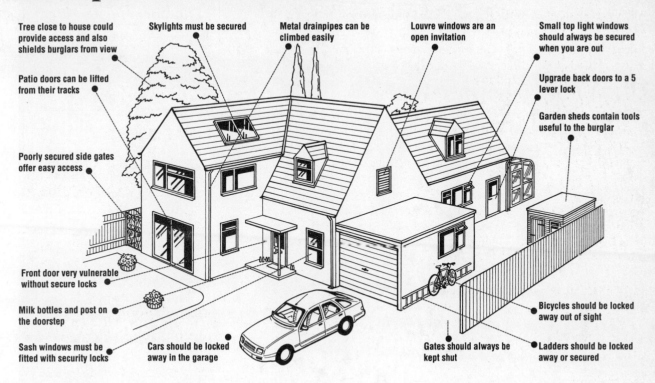

Tree close to house could provide access and also shields burglars from view

Patio doors can be lifted from their tracks

Poorly secured side gates offer easy access

Front door very vulnerable without secure locks

Milk bottles and post on the doorstep

Sash windows must be fitted with security locks

Skylights must be secured

Cars should be locked away in the garage

Metal drainpipes can be climbed easily

Louvre windows are an open invitation

Small top light windows should always be secured when you are out

Upgrade back doors to a 5 lever lock

Garden sheds contain tools useful to the burglar

Bicycles should be locked away out of sight

Gates should always be kept shut

Ladders should be locked away or secured

A Closed Shop

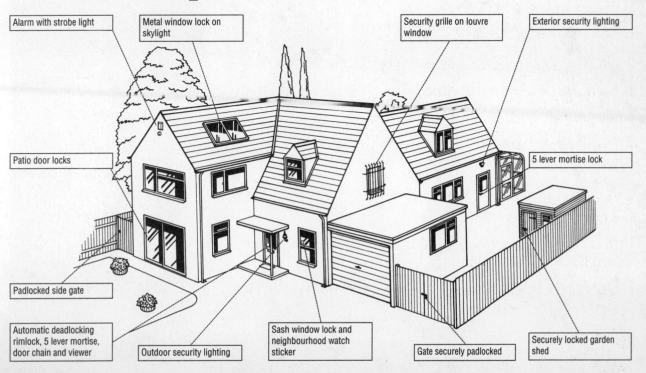

Alarm with strobe light

Metal window lock on skylight

Security grille on louvre window

Exterior security lighting

Patio door locks

5 lever mortise lock

Padlocked side gate

Automatic deadlocking rimlock, 5 lever mortise, door chain and viewer

Outdoor security lighting

Sash window lock and neighbourhood watch sticker

Gate securely padlocked

Securely locked garden shed

Chapter 1

Securing the Home

Doors

For most people, the front door is where security starts. Indeed, one of the first things we should do when we move house is to change the front door lock. However, there are other things we should consider even before that.

Take a good look at the door frame. Make sure it is firmly secured to the surrounding wall, that it isn't rotting or warped and that it is fixed at the sides at intervals of no more than 60cm (2') as well as at the head and threshold, if possible.

Now look carefully at the door. It should be at least 44mm (1¾") thick and preferably of solid wood. The door stile - the depth of solid wood you have available to cut into from the edge of the door to the centre of the keyhole - should be at least 11.9cm (4¾") to allow room for a security mortise lock. If it is less than this but over 92mm (3⅝"), you will need to fit a narrow-stile lock.

Unfortunately, many homes, especially flats, have been fitted with cheap, hollow egg-shell or plywood doors which give way easily under a hefty kick, let alone more forcible attack. You should replace these doors, or anything that you think looks flimsy. Replace them with ones that have a solid hardwood core or, even better, with wood laminate doors (a sandwich of ply and other wood) with little or no glass and preferably without panels, particularly in the lower section. These panels are often only made of plywood and are easily kicked in.

Glass panels inevitably reduce security and, if possible, should be removed or replaced with laminated glass which is much stronger and safer. (See pp.30 on 'Glazing'.)

The letter box in the door should be the minimum size recommended by the Post Office – 38mm x 25cm (1½" x 10"), so that a hand cannot reach in and open the lock from the inside.

A door viewer is an excellent precaution, along with a door chain, and these are covered in Chapter 2.

Three strong hinges should be fitted to the front door and, on outward opening doors, fit hinge bolts mid-way between the hinges. The bolts help prevent the door being levered off its hinges from outside if the hinge pins are successfully removed.

Back and side doors

Back and side doors are often weakly built and inadequately secured, with only an inferior two or three-lever lock. Being out of sight, they provide an easy way in for the casual thief – 62% of all burglaries occur at the rear of property, while the rear or side door is the point of entry in 23% of cases.

Once again, fit hinge bolts to prevent the burglar removing the pins in the hinges, and fit key-operated surface mounted or mortise bolts to the top and bottom of the inside of the door. Don't rely on the sliding bolts so often fitted.

Reinforcing kits protect against attacks on the lock, and levering.

Extra protection for the mortise door lock from Chubb against forceful attacks.

Reinforcing the doors

There are several ways to reinforce the door, door frame and door lock. Frames can be reinforced with steel sections, and doors themselves can be given additional protection with vandal- and attack-resistant facings – either steel, laminates of wood or plywood and glass reinforced plastic (GRP), a particularly tough material. These are sometimes incorporated as a layer beneath a wood veneer so that, on the face of it, the door looks perfectly normal.

A London bar is a steel strip which fits the entire length of the door, protecting the rim lock on one side and reinforcing the frame on the hinge side. It is designed to spread the force of an attack – something a multi-point locking system (a series of three or more locks operated simultaneously from one point) will also do.

Some multi-point systems can be mortised into a new or existing door by a specially trained locksmith, and there is a surface-mounted kit on the market which locks in three points and incorporates a door chain. It needs a door stile of at least 10cm (4") and a visible door frame of at least 35mm (1½") width.

There are also reinforcement kits designed to fit around the lock area and protect it from attack. You can find anti-tamper and lockable letter boxes, some of which are designed to resist arson attacks. The lock itself can be protected with special reinforcement kits.

Locks

There is a wide variety of door locks available but the two main types are rim locks (which are surface-mounted) and mortise locks (which are set into the solid wood and involve chiselling out a section of the door).

On its own, an ordinary rim night latch with a standard cylinder offers little security. It is too easily opened by an intruder if the inside knob can be reached and is vulnerable to manipulation – a strip of plastic or a credit card slid between the door and frame could easily force back the bolt.

A deadlocking rim lock (night latch) is automatically deadlocked when the door is closed and the knob inside can be locked from inside or outside. The knob is then released by turning the key from the outside.

Such locks have hardened steel bolts which are resistant to hacksaw attacks and the lock case and cylinder are, in high security models, protected from drilling, wrenching and other forceful attacks.

An insecure rim lock can usually be replaced by a security version on wooden doors without too much additional woodwork and, being surface mounted, is relatively easy to fit. Look for a model with a box strike, which prevents the bolt being jemmied back into the lock case, and with concealed fixing screws.

There are models for standard and narrow stile (approximately 40mm (1⅝") from edge of door to centre of keyhole) and suitable for varying thicknesses of door. Measure the stile and thickness of your door before choosing the lock.

The mortise lock is concealed within the door and the best carry a kite-mark, to show they meet with BS36211, required by many insurance companies. The British Standard specifies a minimum of five levers with measures to prevent picking, dead-locking to prevent handles and knobs from operating, a bolt which projects at least 14mm (⅝") when it is locked, and anti-drill plates fitted to protect the lock body. Fixing screws must be concealed or inoperable when the door is locked.

Surface-mounted, an automatic deadlocking rim lock is relatively easy to fit yourself. This is Chubb's 4L74.

Yale's PBS1 automatic deadlocking rim lock which has the BS3621 kitemark.

A rim lock with a built-in door restraint, which engages automatically every time the door is opened, is ideal for people on their own, or the elderly. This is Yale's 93 'Checklock'.

The mortise lock is either a deadlock with one hefty hardened steel bolt, usually fitted on a front door along with a rim night latch to reinforce security, or a mortise sashlock which is operated by a handle on one or both sides of the door. This is ideal for back or side doors.

This type of lock will have a latch bolt and a deadlock (*see illustrations*). Once again various attack-resistant features improve the security of these locks, and narrow stile versions are available for use with glazed doors which cannot accommodate the regular size. They are usually 63mm (2½") or 75mm (3") wide and should not be fitted to a door less than 42mm (1⅝") thick.

Since 1957, British lever locks have been made to the same overall size, with spindle and keyhole in the same place, so mortise locks are reasonably easy to replace.

Fitting a mortise door lock

If you move into a new home, you should always change the locks and upgrade them if necessary – you never know who has copies of the old keys. A mortise lock is fitted within the door frame and the best – with at least five levers – meet British Standard BS3621 required by insurance companies.

A mortise deadlock contains a single hardened steel bolt, operated by the key, ideal for front doors, while a mortise sashlock also incorporates a handle on one or both sides of the door and is often used to protect rear and side doors.

> ▶ **SEE PAGE 14 FOR STEP-BY-STEP INSTRUCTIONS ON FITTING A MORTISE DOOR LOCK**

All types of cylinders are available to enable all the locks to be operated by a single key. A system can include padlocks and front door locks. If a key is lost, simply change the cylinder – not the entire lock.

These locks are said to deadlock, to prevent picking, and incorporate anti-drill plates and concealed fixing screws. Narrow versions are available for glazed doors and reinforcement kits will further protect them from attack. Mortise locks should not be fitted to a door less than 42mm (1⅝") thick.

Chubb's 3G115 five-lever mortise deadlock is suitable if you are also fitting an automatic deadlocking rim lock on the front door, and will cost less than the BS version.

A cylinder-operated mortise sash lock for doors where a handle is required for opening from the inside.

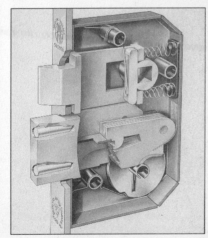

Inside a five lever mortise lock.

High security cylinder locks

The cylinder lock is used throughout Europe and is beginning to be far more widely available here - the traditional British mortise lock is hardly used elsewhere. Cylinder locks will also be the basis of new European Standards.

So, if you are looking for a higher level of key security plus the convenience of replacing a cylinder rather than the entire lock if a key is lost, it has many advantages. The cylinder also allows you to use the same key for the front and back door locks, and even for key-operated window locks.

High security cylinders, available for both mortise locks (look for the Euro-profile cylinder models) and rim locks both use registered keys. This means copies can only be obtained from the manufacturer or from a specially appointed locksmith on confirmation of the user's signature.

Knowing that a lost key cannot easily be duplicated in any keycutting kiosk and that you can continue to use the existing lock case, you might consider the extra expense worthwhile. Often cylinders alone can be fitted to your existing locks, so check with your local locksmith first.

French doors and patio doors

These need special attention. The ideal type of lock for French doors is either a surface-mounted bolt or mortise bolts fitted to the top and bottom of the door, locking into the head of the frame and down into the sill.

The aluminium framed patio door is particularly vulnerable because it is all too easily levered out of the frame. While some manufacturers are improving the security of double-glazed units, it is best to fit a purpose-made patio door lock.

Fitting a patio lock to an aluminium door

As already mentioned, it is best to fit a purpose-made patio door lock - the ideal type is either a surface-mounted bolt or a mortise bolt, fitted top and bottom of the door to engage the head of the frame and the sill.

Care is needed when fitting these as the sliding mechanism and glass may be very close when drilling the holes for the lock. You may have to re-position the lock to avoid drilling through the wheels or another section of the rolling gear. The glass may also be very close to the runners.

Look for a lock with a push bolt and concealed fixing screws which only needs a key to unlock it. Anti-theft devices are also available but check that the width of your door rail is suitable.

▶ **SEE PAGE 20 FOR STEP-BY-STEP INSTRUCTIONS ON FITTING A PATIO LOCK TO AN ALUMINIUM DOOR**

Particularly useful for wooden patio doors where you need more track clearance, ERA's multi-purpose bolt can be fitted to large windows, doors and even garage doors.

A digital lock which operates mechanically using a four digit code.

An easy to install, simple to operate electronic digital lock – the Touchlock comprises everything you need to transform your existing front door lock. Shown is an electric strike, for either mortise or rim lock, a transformer and power supply. The keypad is self-contained and allows you to program your own code.

Digital locks

There is a growing choice in locks which operate using a digital code. Usually the code is four numbers, just like a credit card PIN code, which you can change whenever you like. Some digital products are purely mechanical, operating a deadbolt, while others combine mechanical and electric operation.

Alternatively there are systems which depend entirely on electronic operation. Any system that uses electronics will need an electric strike which incorporates the release mechanism, usually operated through a 12v electrical supply, which will need to be wired separately.

Sometimes a transformer is included in the kit so that the digital unit can be plugged into the mains, or you will need to wire it direct into the power supply. More and more battery-operated systems are coming on to the market which enable the lock unit to remember codes and any other programming facilities it offers.

Perhaps the simplest system is the mains-operated version. Typically, it requires only three cables for connection, is packaged as a kit with a transformer, rim electric release and mortise plate (allowing you to adapt your existing lock to an electric one) plus a slimline keypad which handles all the programming. The keypad can also be linked to a new or existing doorbell.

Ordinary five lever mortise locks and electronic access control systems can be linked to an alarm system, or even security lighting, using a microswitch fitted in the strike. Ask your locksmith to advise you on the right lock to buy. You'd be surprised how a simple door lock can be adapted.

LOCKS AND KEYS
WATCH POINTS

1 **If you move house, change the locks immediately**. You never know who may still have keys that fit.

2 Ladies – **don't keep your house keys in a handbag** when you are out. Put them in a separate jacket pocket or purse.

3 If you are always losing your keys and having to change the locks, think about fitting a **high security cylinder lock**. Then you can just have the cylinder changed.

4 Have keys cut by a good locksmith. Some, but not all, keycutting outlets use inferior blanks which may break. **A locksmith uses the correct equipment** and will produce a good quality, well-finished key that will work.

5 **Never leave spare keys under a doormat or flowerpot** – that's where the thief will look first. And never hang a key inside the letterbox.

6 **Never mark your keys with your name and address**.

Fitting a mortise door lock

A mortise lock is fitted within the door frame and the best makes – with at least five levers – meet British Standard BS3621 required by insurance companies.

A mortise deadlock contains a single hardened steel bolt, operated by the key, ideal for front doors, while a mortise sashlock also incorporates a handle on one or both sides of the door and is often used to protect rear and side doors.

These locks are said to deadlock, to prevent picking, and incorporate anti-drill plates and concealed fixing screws. Narrow versions are available for glazed doors and reinforcement kits will further protect them from attack.

Mortise locks should not be fitted to doors less than 42mm (1⅝") thick.

TOOLS AND MATERIALS

☐ Hand drill + a range of wood bits
☐ Mallet
☐ Chisels – 6mm (¼in) & 12mm (½in)
☐ File – (10mm) ⅜in round
☐ Screwdrivers
☐ Wood glue
☐ Tape measure
☐ Pincers
☐ Pencil

We fitted Ingersoll's M50 British Standard five-lever mortise lock in place of a three-lever lock. It has a hardened deadlocking bolt, 1,500 key combinations and a solid steel box locking plate.

1 Unscrew the face plate, turn the lock to the locked position, hold the bolt firmly with a pair of pincers and carefully pull out the old lock.

2 When replacing a lock, it is advisable to ensure that the distance from the centre of the keyhole to the face plate is the same.

3 Mark the top and bottom of the fore-end carefully and chisel out so that the fore-end fits flush to the wood.

4 With the new lock in the locked position, slide it into the mortise, look through the keyhole and check that the alignment is correct.

5 You can now see how the keyhole and the new lock are going to line up. If necessary, fill odd holes with a small wedge of glued wood.

6 Mark with a pencil if you need to adjust the hole in the door. If it isn't wide enough, the key may bind.

7 If necessary, use a 10mm (⅜in) file to enlarge the hole, clearing out any bits of sawdust from the mortise afterwards.

8 Using a 3mm (⅛in) drill (larger for hard woods), drill pilot holes for the fore-end. Screw the lock into position with the screws provided.

9 If the door opens inwards, fit the keyhole flap on the inside so it isn't trapped in the door stop. With the key in the lock, mark the screw holes and screw the escutcheon into place.

10 Fit the strike plate accurately or the door will be a loose fit. With the lock in the locked position, gently close the door, marking the door jamb where the bolt touches.

11 Holding the striker over the exposed bolt, measure from its edge to the outside of the door. This will give you the outer position of the striker. Make sure that the door shuts fully.

12 Mark the recess and chisel out allowing for the thickness of the striker plate. But remember, if you make a hash of it, it can be difficult to recover!

13 Don't rush to make the screw holes. If it's not right and the door doesn't close correctly you will have to fill them in again.

14 Close the door with the strike in position and make any adjustments at this point. Then drill the pilot holes and insert the screws to hold the face plate in position.

Fitting a rim lock

A surface-mounted rim lock is quite straightforward to fit yourself.
A deadlocking rim lock (night latch) is automatically deadlocked when the
door is closed and the knob inside can be locked from inside or outside. The
knob is then released by turning the key from the outside. Such locks have
hardened steel bolts which are resistant to hacksaw attacks and the lock case
and cylinder are, in high security models, protected from drilling, wrenching
and other forceful attacks. An insecure rim lock can usually be replaced by a
security version on wooden doors without too much additional woodwork
and, being surface mounted, is relatively easy to fit. Look for a model with a
box strike, which prevents the bolt being jemmied back into the lock case,
and with concealed fixing screws.

TOOLS AND MATERIALS

- ☐ Hand drill + a range of wood bits
- ☐ Mallet
- ☐ Chisels – 6mm (¼in) & 12mm (½in)
- ☐ Screwdrivers
- ☐ Tape measure
- ☐ Pincers
- ☐ Square
- ☐ Pencil

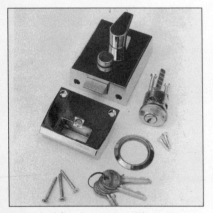

As we had fitted a good quality mortise lock, we chose a middle price range Union Night Latch to complement it. More expensive automatic deadlocking locks are also available.

1 This is the sorry specimen we had to remove first which offered virtually no security by itself.

2 Remove the old lock and remove the old cylinder from the outside of the door. Take care not to damage the door in the process.

3 Carefully check that the new cylinder will fit securely and comfortably in the old cylinder hole.

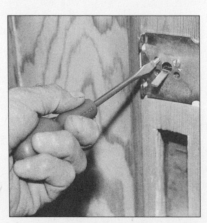

4 Holding the cylinder in place, screw the back plate into position. The lock should fit flush to the door.

5 You will have to cut the tail to the right length. As it is in sections you can snap them off with a pair of pliers. It will need to protrude about 15mm (⅝in).

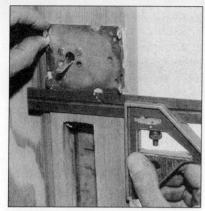

6 Check that the back plate is square, and knock it gently into position with a soft hammer or your hands.

7 Offer up the lock body. Check the manufacturers' instructions and turn the follower (the round bit) using a screwdriver so it is in the right position.

8 Dab a little drop of Loctite or paint on the thread of the screws to prevent them shaking loose and screw the lock case into position.

9 Before positioning the lock's box strike, take care to make sure that the door shuts flush.

10 Offer the striker up to the jamb and mark for the recess (the lip will need to be accommodated).

11 With a soft hammer, carefully knock the striker into the recess you have chiselled out.

12 Before drilling the screw holes, ensure the door will shut snugly, but adjusting if it is too tight.

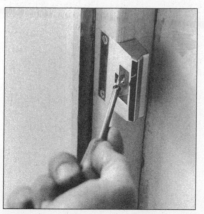

13 An additional angled screw provides greater security and helps pull the box strike square.

14 Seen from the outside, the rim lock cylinder and box strike.

Fitting a mortise bolt

With its hardened steel bolt, resistant to hacksaw attack, and elementary key, the mortise bolt provides a simple yet effective means of securing back and side doors – a favourite way in for the casual thief.

If you have an integral garage, the door leading from the garage to the house should also be secured as a back door – with a five-lever mortise lock and mortise bolts.

Mortise bolts are set into the solid wood and involve chiselling out a section of the door. Ideally, you should fit two bolts, one top and bottom of the door, with particularly vulnerable doors further strengthened by hinge bolts to prevent the burglar removing the pins in the hinges. (See page 29).

TOOLS AND MATERIALS

- ☐ Power drill + a range of wood bits
- ☐ 10mm (⅜in) drill bit (auger)
- ☑ Mallet
- ☐ Chisel – 6mm (¼in)
- ☐ Screwdrivers
- ☐ Tape measure
- ☐ Pincers
- ☐ Pencil

We fitted Chubb's 8002 door mortise bolt. Ideally fit two.

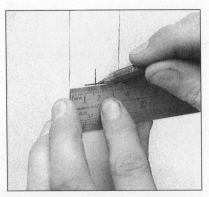

1 Mark the central position of the bolt on the door, approximately 15cm (6″) down from the top in this case.

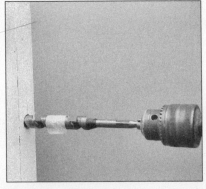

2 Drill a 16mm (⅝in) diameter hole for the bolt. Marking the drill bit with a piece of masking tape or similar will prevent you drilling in too far as this type of drill bit used with a power drill tends to draw itself in before you know where you are!

3 Offer up the lock to ensure it fits the hole correctly, and to position face plate.

4 Mark position of face plate top and bottom.

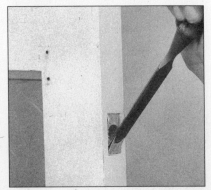

5 Chisel out recess so that the plate fits flush in the wood.

6 To find correct place to drill for key-hole, hold bolt flush with the face of the door, insert key and give it a tap with a hammer. Make sure it is positioned on the inside of the door.

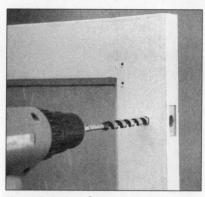

7 Drill a 10mm (⅜in) diameter hole with a 10mm (⅜in) drill bit (also known as an auger drill). Just drill through until you meet the horizontal hole (you won't need to drill very hard).

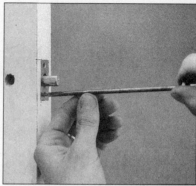

8 Knock the bolt firmly into position in the mortise with a hammer and, using a bradawl, mark the pilot holes for the face plate and screw it into place.

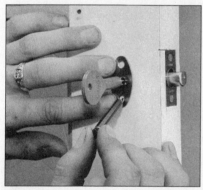

9 To fit the escutcheon on the inside of the door, line it up with the 10mm (⅜in) hole with the key in position. Then mark screw holes with a pencil or bradawl.

10 Drill the holes for the escutcheon's screws rather than simply screwing them in which may result in them going off-line.

11 Screw the escutcheon plate into place. Then, having checked that the lock works correctly, shoot the bolt with the door closed so that it marks the door jamb.

12 Drill the door jamb, using a 16mm (⅝in) drill bit, for the bolt engagement hole.

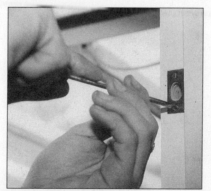

13 Fit the face plate, recessing it as described above.

14 The mortise bolt fitted and in the locked position, ready for the key to be placed somewhere safe!

Fitting a patio lock to an aluminium door

The aluminium framed patio door is particularly vulnerable because it can easily be levered out of the frame. It is best to fit a purpose-made patio door lock – the ideal type is either a surface-mounted bolt or a mortise bolt, fitted top and bottom of the door to engage the head of the frame and the sill.

Care is needed when fitting these as the sliding mechanism and glass may be very close when drilling the holes for the lock. You may have to re-position the lock to avoid drilling through the wheels or another section of the rolling gear. The glass may also be very close to the runners.

Look for a lock with a push bolt and concealed fixing screws which only needs a key to unlock it. Anti-theft devices are also available but check that the width of your door rail is suitable.

TOOLS AND MATERIALS

- ☐ Power drill + a range of metal bits
- ☐ Hammer
- ☐ Screwdrivers
- ☐ Centre punch

Sixty-four per cent of burglars break in through the rear of a property.

We fitted Chubb's 8K119 patio door lock. It uses a convenient push-to-lock mechanism and a key to unlock. It is best to fit one top and bottom.

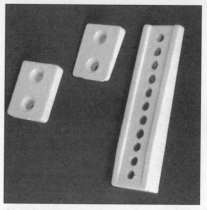

If not properly secured, patio doors can be levered off their tracks, so fit an anti-lift device if possible but check first that the width of your door rail is suitable.

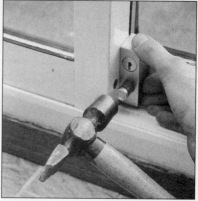

1 Holding the lock snugly against the central vertical frame where the two doors meet, turn the key clockwise to release the bolt and tap the end of the bolt so it leaves a slight indent on the frame.

2 If the mark is not distinct enough, use a centre punch. Remember, you may be drilling close to the sliding mechanism and have to re-position the lock. Work with extreme care.

3 Start drilling the hole for the bolt with a small bit. Take care not to drill through the wheels or rolling gear. The glass may also be very close to the runners.

4 Build up to the larger 10mm (⅜in) drill required to make the final hole and clean out the metal swarf afterwards.

5 Mark, punch and drill the holes for the fixing screws in the side of the door, using a 3.4mm (⅛in) drill, and make sure you don't touch the glass and shatter it.

6 Re-position the lock with the bolt out and the door open so you can screw the self-tapping screws firmly into place. A drop of lubricant will help them locate more securely.

7 To lock, simply push the bolt home - the mechanism is self-locking but you will need a key to release the bolt.

Windows

In more than half of all reported break-ins, burglars have gained access through a downstairs window. And, in a lot of instances, they haven't even had to force their way in – they have come in through an open window. Proof, if that were needed, that windows which are easy to reach, no matter how small, should never be left open when the home is unoccupied.

When securing your home, windows must be one of your first considerations. In reality, a determined thief could probably defeat most window locks but the majority of break-ins are committed by the opportunist – and the last thing he wants is to spend a lot of time breaking into a house. He is more interested in a quick entry and exit to reduce the chances of being caught!

If you own a recently-built house it is quite likely that window locks have already been installed. Homes built to standards laid down by the National House-Building Council (NHBC) will have key-operated locks fitted to all downstairs windows and others which are readily accessible.

This requirement became law in 1989, but if you are uncertain about the locks fitted to your windows, a quick call to your Crime Prevention Officer at the local police station should put your mind at rest.

The traditional window fasteners fitted in older houses offer very little protection. Smash a small area of glass, slip a hand in, release the catch and your possessions are there for the taking – conveniently carried out through the door. It's easier still if the catch can be forced or slipped from the outside.

The purpose of fitting window locks is to prevent incidents such as these occurring. A vast number of locks are available from DIY multiples, hardware stores and security locksmiths to suit all types of windows, and all are relatively inexpensive.

But first, you'll need to take a look at what type of windows you have. Are they made from wood or metal (steel or aluminium)? How do they open – are they hinged or sliding? Also take a note of the width of the stile or rail where the lock will be fitted. Finally, take a good look at the frames.

Window locks fitted to rotten wooden frames or poorly fitting windows will provide little protection, and these areas will have to be attended to first, either by strengthening, repairing, or replacing windows and frames. Make sure that window putty is in good condition, too. Dried out putty is easily removed, allowing the glass to be lifted out.

You will then need to check how many window locks are required. All downstairs windows should be secured (including basement windows) and any upstairs windows which could be reached by a flat roof, wall, drainpipe or anything that a burglar could climb. Casement windows which are 1m (3') high or more, or sash windows 1m (3') wide should be secured with two window locks.

Choose carefully – consider how often each window is used, whether it may need to be used as an exit in the case

The Chubb 8K100 for wood or metal framed windows.

The ERA Securistay allows windows to be opened slightly for ventilation, but not sufficiently wide for a child to fall through.

Cockspur handles are easily replaced with locking versions like this one from ERA.

of a fire, and also who will operate the locks. An elderly person might need locks which are specially designed for easy operation. If there are children in the house, you may prefer to install locks in their room which enable the windows to be opened for ventilation but not wide enough for a child to fall out.

If you are in any doubt, remember that advice is available from Crime Prevention Officers and security locksmiths who will have a range of locks and can recommend those to suit your particular requirements.

Casement windows

Casement windows may be hinged at the side or top, or pivot vertically or horizontally, and usually secured with a cockspur handle. This is easily replaced with a locking cockspur – readily available and quite secure providing the handle cannot be removed. A higher degree of security can be obtained, particularly on larger windows, when the window is actually locked to the frame. Locks that secure the window latch or catch could, in a deter- mined attack, be levered apart.

There are many variations but only two types of window lock – mortise and surface-mounted. Mortise locks are neat and unobtrusive but are certainly more difficult to fit and may be more fiddly to operate. Fitting requires the removal of wood. On narrow frames, this could weaken the frame. All locks, whether mortise or surface-mounted, must be fitted accurately to be really secure, with holes drilled to the exact size.

Surface-mounted locks are easier to fit and provide a greater choice of style, strength and price. However, surface-mounted locks do rely on their fixings for

strength and any fixing screws which are still visible when the lock is secured should be drilled out or burred over, so they cannot be unscrewed.

When installing window locks, take care not to insert screws too near to the glass which is recessed in the frame, otherwise the window may crack. Bear in mind, also, that striking plates may have to be mortised into the frame. The lock's packaging should provide detailed fitting instructions and dimensions. Window locks are often sold in packs of four or six and supplied with a key to operate all the locks. Additional keys are available if you want them.

Probably the simplest locks to operate are those which lock automatically every time the window is closed, or those which have a button you push to lock, and use a key to unlock – so there's no excuse for not locking the windows every time you leave the house. Other surface- mounted locks have a special key which screws the lock shut and is used again to unscrew it.

Fanlights

Never make the mistake of thinking that a fanlight is too small to allow access. It can allow a thief to tamper with locks fitted to the larger window and remember – the opportunist burglar could be a youth or small child!

Fanlights are kept closed with a stay which provides very little security. They can be secured with a casement stay, stop or screw, but ideally you should fit a surface- mounted casement-style lock which secures the window to the frame. There are also locks which enable a fanlight to be locked in a slightly open position to provide ventilation.

For convenience, the ERA Snaplock locks automatically when the window is closed.

Chubb's WS1 secures a sash window in the fully closed position, or slightly open for ventilation.

The Chubb 8K106 is easily fitted to steel and most aluminium-framed hinged windows.

Sash windows

Sash windows, consisting of two windows which slide up and down, are commonly found in older properties and often provide easy access. The major manufacturers provide locks specifically for sash windows. Particularly useful is a locking stop which allows the window to be secured in a closed or slightly open position. Bolts and screw locks are also available. A cheap and effective method of further improving security on a sash window is to cut a broomstick to fit tightly in the sash channel. This could only be removed if the glass is broken.

Louvre windows

Louvre windows are particularly vulnerable because the glass slats can easily be removed. Ideally they should be replaced with more conventional windows, but if cost prohibits this, glue each slat in place with a strong epoxy resin. A grille or shutter fitted over the window provides much greater protection.

Rooflights and skylights can also permit entry, particularly if they are accessible from a flat roof. If they cannot be secured easily with locks, consider installing window bars, or a grille.

Metal frames

All the major manufacturers provide surface-mounted locks specifically for metal window frames but installation is slightly more difficult than for wooden frames as it requires the drilling of holes in thin strips of metal and special screws for aluminium. If in doubt about the installation of locks, call in a locksmith.

Locks for metal windows may secure the cockspur handle by stopping the handle being opened; they may fit on to the opening window and are secured by locking against the fixed frame; they may operate on a 'swing lock' principle similar to a lock for a wooden window; and there are also locks available to secure metal sliding windows which work on a similar principle to a patio door lock.

Keys

Window locks are normally supplied with a universal key which fits all locks of the same type. This is helpful in some ways, enabling you to purchase as many keys as you want, but it also inevitably reduces the degree of security which window locks provide. Having said that, it's important to remember that most break-ins are committed by opportunists and the sight of window locks will probably send them scuttling off in search of an easier target. Also, with the wide range of locks available on the market, the burglar would have to carry a huge bunch of keys around with him to make sure that he had the right key to release your window.

If you live in a high risk area, however, some major manufacturers, do offer window locks with the option of high security keys. This does increase security but also means you will have to go back to the manufacturer or specialist locksmith should you lose the keys!

Double glazing

Double glazing can in itself improve security. Well-fitted units prevent catches from being slipped and leave the burglar with two (or more) panes of glass to break rather than just one. In particularly vulnerable areas, laminated glass could be installed for greater security (see p.31).

UPVC units are normally supplied with security locks built in and these often feature multi-point locking systems which shoot bolts into the frame all around the window to provide a high degree of security. However, if you are installing double glazing, you need to take care and use a reputable firm.

In UPVC and aluminium window units, suitable fixings must be used to ensure that the glass cannot be removed externally unless it is actually broken. External beading can be removed in seconds, allowing the entire pane of glass to be lifted out. External glazing beads should be 'security glazing beads', which cannot be removed without special tools. Alternatively the glass may be bonded to the frame or secured with glass retaining clips. Internal glazing beads should be designed to resist being dislodged by external impact.

The last thing you want, of course, is to make your home look like a fortress. Window locks are, in most cases, unobtrusive and these days are available in a wide choice of finishes, including white, brass, chrome and brown, to suit all types of property.

Appearance, obviously, will be a consideration but it is far more important to choose locks which are easy to use and offer the degree of security you require. You may have to pay a bit more but it will be money well spent.

WINDOW
WATCHPOINTS

1	Fit locks to **all accessible windows**, including fanlights.
2	Make sure you know **exactly what you need** before you buy.
3	Locks should secure the **window** to the **actual frame**.
4	Frames and windows **must be in good condition**.
5	If you have any doubts, ask a **Crime Prevention Officer** or security specialist.
6	Surface-mounted locks require slightly less DIY expertise.
7	Choose locks that are **easy to operate**, so you'll use them.
8	**Louvre windows are vulnerable and should be replaced.**
9	Locks with **high security keys** provide **greater protection**, particularly for high risk areas.
10	Check for optional/standard security features on **double-glazed windows**.

Fitting a metal window lock

When securing your home, windows must be one of your first considerations. The last thing the opportunist thief wants is to spend a lot of time breaking into a house. He is more interested in a quick entry and exit to reduce the chances of being caught! The purpose of fitting window locks is to prevent this happening.

Traditional window fasteners offer very little protection. If you are uncertain about the locks fitted to your windows, call your local Crime Prevention Officer.

A vast range of locks is available to suit all types of windows, all relatively inexpensive. All downstairs windows should be secured (including basement windows) and any easily reached upstairs windows.

TOOLS AND MATERIALS

- ☐ Power drill
- ☐ Drill bit & sleeve included in kit
- ☐ Safety glasses
- ☐ Chisels – 6mm (¼in) & 12mm (½in)
- ☐ Screwdrivers
- ☐ Pencil
- ☐ Centre punch

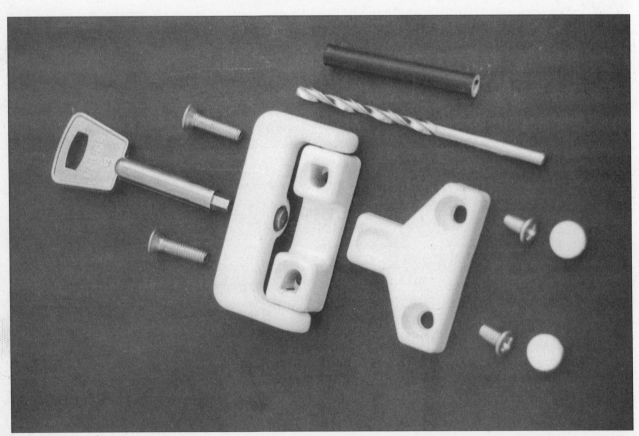

We fitted Chubb's 8K106, specially designed for metal windows and supplied with drill bit and self-tapping screws. The key supplied will also operate Chubb's 8K101 for wooden windows. You may need to chisel out some wood from the surrounding frame to fit this type of lock, particularly if the window doesn't shut flush. It's also a good idea to wear safety glasses when drilling metal.

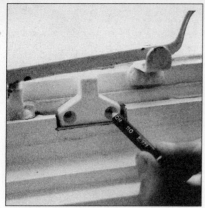

1 With the window open, first mark the screw holes for the lock base unit (the "staple"). Here the wood surround has been cut away to permit flush fit of the staple on the metal frame.

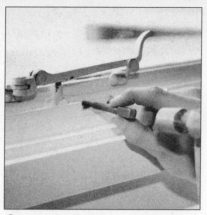

2 Use a centre punch to make a clearer indentation. This will also give the drill something to bite into and stop it going off.

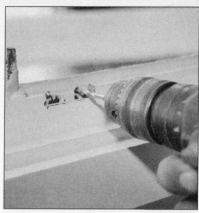

3 Using the drill bit and black sleeve supplied (to indicate how far to drill safely without hitting the glass). Drill the screw holes.

4 Position the staple and screw in place, using the self-tapping screws provided.

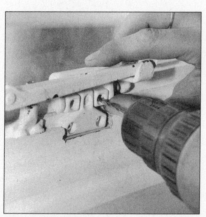

5 With the window closed, sit the lock body on the staple and mark the fixing screw holes.

6 Using the drill plus sleeve, and watching out for the glass, drill the holes for the lock body.

7 Screw the lock body into position.

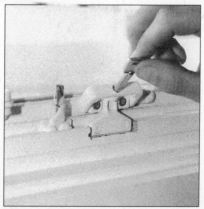

8 The key locates in the lift up section of the lock body and…

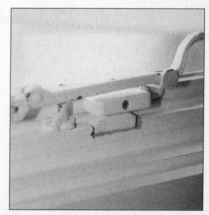

9 …is brought down to lock into position.

Fitting a sash window lock

TOOLS AND MATERIALS

- [ ] Power drill + a range of wood bits
- [ ] 10mm (⅜in) drill bit (auger)
- [ ] Mallet
- [ ] Chisels – 6mm (¼in) & 12mm (½in)
- [ ] Screwdrivers
- [ ] Tape measure
- [ ] Pencil
- [ ] Bradawl

1 We fitted Chubb's 8013 dual screws. You will need two for a standard sash window. These may not be suitable, if there isn't enough overlap to line up or if they close imperfectly. In which case, choose another type of sash lock.

2 To begin, unscrew the removable pin which fits in the bush. The bush will be fixed to the bottom (inside) sash.
Making sure the windows are tightly closed, drill two 10mm (⅜in) holes. To ensure you don't hit the glass, measure the depth of wood to the glass and mark the drill with masking or insulation tape.

3 Using a large screwdriver, screw in the dual screw.

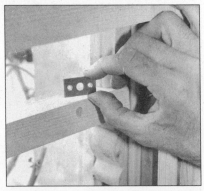

4 Reverse the windows completely so you can get to the bottom of the outer sash and offer up the face plate, finding the central position.

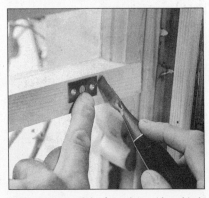

5 Scribe round the face plate with a chisel.

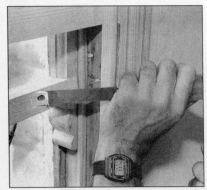

6 Chisel out so the face plate is recessed and flush. Work gently as putty may be loose.

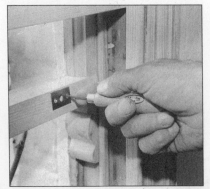

7 Mark position of screws with a bradawl and screw the face plate into place. A ratchet screwdriver is useful here.

8 With windows in closed position, wind in pin with the key provided.

Fitting hinge bolts

We fitted Chubb's WS14 Hinge Bolts to our front door. They are designed to resist forceful attacks and to secure the hinged side of the door. Fit two.

1 Position the bolts approximately 15mm (⅝in)down from the hinges. Drill the door first, making a 10mm (⅜in) hole to a depth of approximately 38mm (1½in) The manufacturer's instructions may specify a smaller hole, but this can result in too tight a fit.

2 Tap stud into hole with a mallet.

3 To find the right position for the hole in the door jamb, gently push the door to with the stud in position. This will leave a small mark on the door jamb and give you your drilling point. Drill a 16mm (⅝in) hole to a depth of approximately 10mm (¾in).

4 Position the face plate centrally over the hole and mark it with a chisel.

5 Pare the wood away around the hole to recess the face plate neatly.

6 Drill the two screw holes ...

7 ... and screw the face plate into position. Make sure the door shuts easily, and fit the second hinge bolt.

Glazing

One of the weakest areas of any building is often its glazing. Glass is very vulnerable. The wrong sort of glass fitted in the wrong place increases the number of weak points in a building. In 21% of all domestic burglaries, the intruder breaks glass to gain entry.

Secure locks and bolts will act as a deterrent – especially against the opportunist – but, if you are considering replacing windows or glazing for reasons of safety or energy efficiency, it may be worth fitting glass which offers greater security in several particularly vulnerable areas.

● Easily accessible ground floor rear windows and doors which are out of sight of neighbours or passers by.
● Louvre windows.
● Glass panels in the front door, or to the side of the door, which allow a burglar to break the glass, put his hand through and release the catch.
● Leaded lights – burglars can gain access by leaning on these to stretch the lead, then lift out the small panes, undo the catch and climb in. Double glazed units with a leaded light effect cannot be attacked like this.

Types of glass:
Annealed glass

In homes, most windows are normally fitted with ordinary annealed glass. Annealed glass (also known as float or plate) breaks very easily, producing long, sharp-edged splinters which can cause horrific injuries. It is very vulnerable to the thief who may break a small area of glass near a lock or handle to gain access. He is less likely to smash a large glazed area as the resulting noise could attract attention.

Wired glass

The appearance of wired glass can be misleading, with the wire mesh making it look stronger than it really is. In most cases it is simply annealed glass with a thin steel mesh embedded. The glass is easily fractured but the mesh is designed to hold the glass in place, acting as a barrier until the mesh is sheared.

Once this occurs the glass will just fall away leaving jagged fragments and the additional risk of injury from protruding wires. With sustained pressure, the glazed area can be removed from the surrounding beading. Wired glass is mainly used as a fire retarding material, providing resistance for up to one hour or more in special cases.

There is, however, a safety wired glass which combines fire resistance with impact resistance. This is provided by a specially developed, electrically treated steel wire mesh. It is classified as a Class C safety glazing material in accordance with BS6206 and satisfies the fire requirements of Part B of the Building Regulations.

Toughened glass

Toughened or tempered glass is annealed glass which has been subjected to a heating and fast cooling process to give much greater strength. Greater impact is necessary to

Annealed glass breaks very easily, producing long, sharp-edged splinters which can cause horrific injuries.

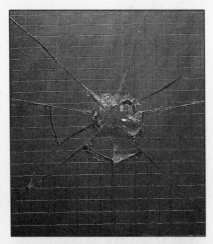

Once wired glass breaks, severe injuries can be caused by sharp splinters and protruding wires.

When broken, toughened glass will shatter into tiny fragments, ensuring that injuries are much less severe.

break it but when it does break, the glass will shatter into tiny pieces. These particles are not sharp like annealed glass so injuries are much less severe but, once broken, it does provide the burglar with a safe entry and exit.

Because of the manufacturing process, toughened glass cannot be cut to size on site and must be ordered to size from a glass merchant. Any measurements, therefore, must be accurate.

Laminated glass

Laminated glass is an excellent safety glass and, unlike other types of glass, can provide a very high level of security depending on the thickness used. It is made by bonding together two or more panes of ordinary float glass, alternated with a plastic interlayer called polyvinyl butyral (PVB).

The outer layer of glass will break almost as easily as ordinary glass, but the pieces remain bonded to the interlayer so there are no dangerous splinters or glass fragments. By using sheer brute force, an intruder may eventually break through the interlayer, depending on the thickness of the glass, but the amount of noise and length of time required should be a sufficient deterrent.

The number of glass and PVB layers is varied according to the application. In the home, laminated glass with a thickness of 6.4mm or 6.8mm (approx. ¼") is most commonly used. This is known as a safety glass, which also incorporates an element of security.

Glass with a thickness of 7.5mm (⁷⁄₁₆") or more is known as security or anti-bandit glass and is used in retail and commercial applications. Anti-bandit glass has thicker interlayers than safety laminated glass and special glazing techniques are usually employed.

Installation

Annealed glass used around the home is normally 4mm (⅛") thick so, when installing laminated glass, the extra thickness must be taken into consideration. When framing; it may prove a problem with existing fixtures.

Laminated glass for use in interior windows and doors can be installed using putty, although laminated glass in exterior installations should be fitted using a silicone-based sealant to prevent moisture penetrating between the glass and frame since moisture can, on rare occasions, cause delamination. Because of its construction, the glass must be cut from both sides. It is as easy to fit as ordinary glass, bearing in mind the thickness and cutting requirements, but you would be well advised to contact a glazier for advice and have the glass cut to size.

Laminated glass offers other benefits, over and above security and safety. These include reducing ultra-violet rays, which cause furnishings to fade, and providing insulation against noise. It can also be used in double glazing. (If only one of the two panes of glass is laminated, this should be installed on the inside of the unit to maximise safety benefits).

The cost of laminated glass differs from glazier to glazier, so it's a good idea to obtain several quotes. Generally, laminated glass costs approximately half as much again as ordinary glass but, when it is installed or replaced complete with new frame and glass, the additional cost of laminated glass will only be 20-30% at most.

Plastic films

An alternative to reglazing is the application of an adhesive plastic film on to an existing pane of glass. These films are designed to cut down the amount of sunlight getting into a room, to reduce heat loss and to make vulnerable areas of glass safer and more secure. Some films offer a one-way mirrored effect to increase privacy, allowing the occupants to see out but preventing anyone looking in from outside.

Films are available in a variety of thicknesses, depending on the degree of protection required – from accidental impact through to vandalism and even terrorist bomb attacks. Buy a good quality film which is scratch resistant and UV stabilised. It should be tested to BS6206. Thinner films are suitable

With laminated glass any shattered fragments adhere to the plastic interlayer, avoiding injury and prohibiting entry.

Laminated glass fitted to easily accessible ground floor windows and doors will deter intruders.

for DIY installation for use around the home and where the area to be covered is not too large. DIY film is available up to 61cm (2') wide – this is considered to be the largest width that should be applied without specialist training.

The installation process is quite simple but it can be difficult to apply the film smoothly. Fitting requires spraying the surface of a previously cleaned pane of glass with water, removing the protective liner and sliding the film on to the wet surface. With some makes, the adhesive does not adhere immediately so the film can be positioned accurately.

A squeegee is then used to iron out air bubbles and excess water. Edges may be trimmed using a straight edge trimming guide and a Stanley knife. Films take about four weeks to dry properly. After that, they should be virtually undetectable.

When buying glass it is advisable to approach a glazier who is a member of the Glass and Glazing Federation. A good glazier will ask you where the glass is to be sited and, if the application is potentially dangerous, should insist that you fit safety glass.

Safety

According to figures released in 1994 by RoSPA (Royal Society for the Prevention of Accidents), 40,000 people have to be treated in hospital every year after accidents in the home involving glass.

With the revised Building Regulations of June 1992, it is now a legal requirement to install safety glazing in certain critical locations. If people are likely to come into contact with glazing while passing through a building, it should: if broken on impact, break in a way which is unlikely to cause injury; resist impact without breaking; be shielded or protected from impact.

These regulations apply to glass which is installed in new buildings, including extensions and conservatories, or in areas where glazing did not exist previously. In homes built before June 1992, it is important to assess the safety of glazing, particularly if there are young children at home.

Check any areas of glass which could be potentially dangerous. This includes internal doors, full length windows, patio doors, porches, conservatories, front and back doors, glass doors at the bottom of stairs, glass-topped tables, full length mirrors and glass roofs and skylights.

If you move to a new home, ask whether safety glass has been installed. Each pane of safety glass should be marked in one of the corners but sometimes the marks can be concealed in the framing. The mark should incorporate the words BS6206, which shows the glass conforms to the relevant British Standard for safety in buildings. It will also feature the letter 'T' for toughened or 'L' for laminated glass, as well as the registration number of the company which supplied the glass. If in doubt, call in a glazier for advice.

If non-safety glass is fitted in potentially dangerous areas, either remove it and replace it with safety glass or place wooden battens across to prevent anyone falling against it. Safety films can also be used but the Glass and Glazing Federation recommend that this should be carried out professionally. If the film is applied correctly, the combination of glass and film can reach BS6206 but check with the supplier that this is the case.

In all cases, remember that some glass or plastic glazing materials can present a serious obstacle to emergency escape. Every room must have a window which can be opened and is large enough to climb through. Keys for security locks must be kept readily to hand.

British Standards

Glazing for Buildings

BS6262 – identifies areas in the home where safety glazing should be installed to reduce the risk of injuries resulting from broken glass.

BS6206 – impact performance for flat safety glass.

BS6206 – was introduced to define a safety glass.

Using an impact performance test devised by the British Standards Institution, a glass is defined as Class A, B or C relating to the level of protection it gives. A, the highest grade, is strong enough to resist the impact of a 14-year-old boy running at the speed of a four-minute mile.

GLASS & GLAZING
WATCHPOINTS

1 Security glass will give **greater protection** on **vulnerable windows and doors**.

2 When buying glass, go to a member of the **Glass and Glazing Federation** (GGF).

3 It is now a **legal requirement** to install **safety glazing** in certain critical locations in new buildings, or areas where glazing did not exist previously.

4 Check glass in your home for marks which illustrate whether it is **safety glass**.

5 Replace any areas of glass which could be **potentially dangerous**, especially if there are young children at home.

6 Make sure that fitted safety films reach **BS6206**.

7 Ensure that each room provides an **emergency escape**.

Grilles and shutters

It may be that you have one or two windows that are just asking for a thief to break in, and window locks simply won't be enough. A patio door, side window out of view or a window looking out over a flat roof may all be candidates for the extra protection of a grille or shutter.

While a grille or shutter is an obvious visual deterrent, you don't want to feel imprisoned in your own home and there is no reason at all why you should. There are many very attractive and effective grilles and shutters available, some of which are designed to be DIY fitted quite easily.

But you must make sure that you are not blocking a means of escape in a fire, although not every window need be considered a potential escape route.

If the grille or shutter does not have to be secured all the time, the answer may be one that slides to one side, concertina fashion. Other kits, especially useful for protecting patio doors and French windows, are simply a series of adjustable bars, ready for you to assemble and fit, which can be left to hang down by the side of the door when you are at home. Alternatively, you can buy units which are designed for individual windows and are quickly removable; either they can be unlocked and lifted away or are collapsible.

Some grilles are secured with a padlock but make sure that both the padlock and its key provide good quality,

strength and security. An integral lock is best, fitted with a clutch bolt, which expands in size when it is in the secure position. This type of lock is far more likely to be used than having to fiddle with a padlock.

A fixed decorative grille would suit a small side window but, if it is fitted outside, beware of providing a thief with a convenient ladder up to another, less well protected window, drainpipe or roof.

Many grilles on the market are perfectly suitable for DIY fitting and are produced as made-to-measure kits. They may be in lattice style or be more decorative, using traditional wrought iron designs in solid steel, clamped together with specially designed rosettes, for example.

Usually the manufacturer or supplier provides you with a grid on which to draw the size of the window together with instructions on how to work out the components you will need. Alternatively, a good locksmith or security centre may well survey the site for you and supply the made up grille for you to fit.

Extra door defence

Often you can adapt these kits to create an outside grille for a complete door or to protect a window panel in the door or to one side, without losing the benefits of light.

Secur + DIY grilles are clamped together with security rosettes. Just order the components you need for the size of window.

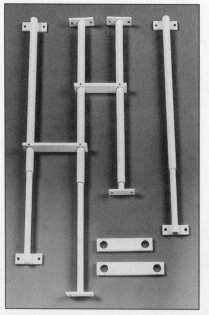

Adjustabars from Baddeley Rose allow you to protect a small or large window and even a glass door.

This expandable lattice grille can be slid to one side when not required.

Alternatively, there are 'secondary' grille doors on the market which are fitted rather like a full-height gate outside the front door, allowing you to open your front door and communicate with callers safely. These can also be used on back doors, to secure porches or alleyways.

It is essential to ensure that a quick exit in an emergency is possible. Some makes are fitted with weak-weld points to enable the fire brigade to release the door rapidly in an emergency. They also have quick-release locking mechanisms allowing immediate exit and security features such as lockable letter box and continuous hinge. This type of door may be fitted with either a key on both sides or a key one side and a protected knob on the inside, to prevent the lock from being hooked open from outside.

Fixtures and fittings

Materials used for bar-based grilles vary. Avoid hollow tubular bars which are usually easy to saw through. A solid, high grade steel or mild steel bar is ideal. The surrounding wall should be sound and the fixings of good quality. (Some kits have security screws and nuts supplied as standard.)

If you are making the grille or having it made for you, make sure the joints are arc-welded, rather than MIG-welded which isn't nearly as strong. Check all the joints because they may simply be spot welded.

Bars and grilles should not be fixed to plastic window frames, even those reinforced with metal, mainly because they are too heavy but also as drilling the frames would probably damage them beyond repair. You could, however, fix them between the window ledges and the window's lintel.

Fixing methods

To fit a grille or bars, you must first decide whether to fit them permanently on the outside or whether to fit them inside and, if necessary, make them removable. Inside will be more secure as it will be harder for the burglar to get at fixing points or attack the grille itself.

Instructions should be given with the kit on how to measure up and fix a grille or bars but here is some guidance on what you will need to do.

Grilles can be face-fixed (i.e. fixed to the window frame or to the face of the inside wall itself) or reveal-

Homeguard grilles can be lifted away from the window and can be fitted with an emergency release lock. Extension arms are telescopic for an accurate fit.

fitted (i.e. fitted to the vertical wall to the side of the window). These will require different fixings, so make sure you tell the manufacturer which you want.

If you are fixing the grille in the reveal, you should have a minimum depth of 95mm (3¾") to allow for the window to be opened; you should also check whether the reveals are splayed at an angle and whether there are any likely obstructions causing an odd-shaped opening – like a fanlight or a sink.

Sometimes the reveal may bulge in the middle so check the width and the height all the way along and make sure you take the smallest measurement. If it does vary too much you may need to use small packing pieces of hard wood (no more than 32mm (1¼") though).

Remember that any protection is only as good as the weakest point. This is often the wall or woodwork to which the grille is fixed, so you should make sure that this is sound before you begin. For example, brickwork can become friable and woodwork can rot. It is some-

times possible to use a two-part epoxy cement to hold the wall plug in a brick wall but deteriorated woodwork should be replaced or some other fixing point found.

If you are fixing the grille to wood, use one-way wood screws – and drill a pilot hole first to ensure you can tighten it easily – it's virtually impossible to reverse them if you make a mistake. The best approach is to get the position right with ordinary screws first and then replace them one at a time with the one-way screws.

If you are attaching the grille to brick, drill and plug the brickwork, avoiding mortar joints, and attach using one-way wood screws. You can treat concrete blockwork in the same way or you could use expansion studs. Make sure the studs are blocked with armour rings to stop them undoing. Don't use an expanding fastener on plaster board or similar hollow walls. It is best to fasten a hardwood batten to the ceiling or walls and fix the grille to that.

Have as many fixing points as possible at regular intervals – this will help to hold the grille rigid – and don't try to fix both ends of a rectangular grille while the long sides are free. If you are using bars, make sure they are no more than 10cm (4") apart. This recommendation is now incorporated in the Building Regulations for child safety, although the requirement for British Standard is 12.5cm (5") and insurance specifications are often somewhere between the two.

Don't use bars which are too long overall or not 'tied' together by a horizontal or some other secure fixing. If they are too long, they could be sprung or distorted with very little effort. If you are fitting bars, remember you will need one less than the number of spaces and it is helpful to have an even number of spaces so that you can have a centre point fixing.

Make sure that the grille or bars you buy are weather resistant – probably epoxy coated – and that any locking devices not only offer good security but are also quick-release if necessary.

A decorative grille could also be used to protect a doorway or patio door. Ensure it does not seal off a potential fire exit though.

The Continental look

Shutters are a completely different concept, offering security, insulation, protection from sunlight and reduction in noise. Privacy, too, may be an important element for people living alone. If, for example, you have a holiday home, shutters can be particularly useful for protection while you are absent.

Rather more complicated to install, they will usually be of aluminium, steel or PVC and will require a box, the width of the window, to be fitted at the head of the window for the shutter to roll into.

While they can be fitted to bay windows, they are not suitable for bow windows or curved frames.

Shutter operation

Although fitted outside, shutters are operated from inside, either by a handle or an electric motor, operated by remote control or by a switch. If they are operated electrically, it may be possible to link them to an alarm system or to a time switch so they can be opened and closed at pre-set times. Shutters are usually made to order and fitted professionally. It is also possible to have the shutters supplied complete with window.

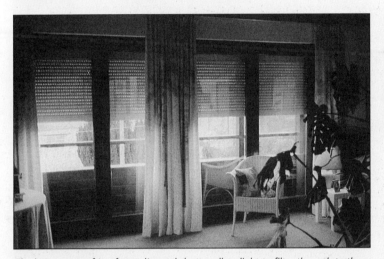

The latest types of 'perforated' metal shutter allow light to filter through to the inside and are available in a variety of colours.

Shutters are ideal for holiday homes, providing privacy and security. They can also protect furnishings from fading in the sunlight.

Chapter 2

Indoor Security
Who's at the door?

Most callers are genuine but, sadly, no-one can afford to be too trusting these days. Beating the doorstep conman need cost very little but common-sense precautions are necessary to ensure that a caller is genuine, and to avoid being pressurised into buying goods or services that you do not really want.

Security devices

The most important point is to ensure that you can see and talk to the caller before opening the door and putting yourself at risk. If the front door or nearby windows do not provide a good view of the caller, you should install a door viewer.

Simple to fit and unobtrusive once in place, it comprises a wide-angle lens which normally provides a viewing angle of between 160° and 190°, enabling you to see the caller clearly, even if he or she is standing to one side.

The installation of a porch light, which comes on automatically or can be switched on from indoors, will ensure that callers are clearly visible after dark or in shadow.

The front door should also be fitted with a door chain or limiter. This prevents the door being opened more than a fraction – just enough for you to talk to the caller and check credentials or sign for a package or letter without allowing him in.

To be of real use, however, the chain must be strong and should be secured with screws that are at least 30mm (1¼") long. A door limiter is often of more solid construction, utilising a steel bar rather than a chain, and offers greater resistance if someone tries to force their way in.

An alternative device is screwed to the bottom of the door and worked by pressing your foot against a lever. This allows the householder to secure the door quickly in a partially open position and enables the door to be pushed closed again but stops any attempt to force it further open.

Some personal attack alarms – which can be triggered in the event of an attack to sound an ear-piercing screech – are sold with wall mounting brackets and can be kept conveniently near the front door. In the event of someone trying to force their way in, the alarm can easily be triggered to alert neighbours or passers-by.

Once the door viewer and door limiter are in place, don't forget to use them. Conmen are crafty and will use numerous tricks to try to force their way into your home. And it's not only male callers you must be wary of - people have also fallen victim to female and child confidence tricksters.

Communal entrances

Many blocks of flats these days utilise 'entry-phone' systems to ensure a greater degree of security. If you let someone into your flat, you cannot always be sure that he actually leaves the building afterwards. Once a

Fitting a door viewer ...

... and a door chain are both simple, inexpensive precautions, and they will make you feel safer.

criminal gains entry to the block, he can easily go from flat to flat unchallenged until he finds one to break into.

If the caller is a stranger, it is best to play safe and either refuse admittance or, at the very least, escort him off the premises. For the same reasons, never hold the door open for a stranger who arrives when you are entering or leaving the building. For additional security, fit a door viewer and door limiter to your flat door so you can still refuse admittance when necessary.

Dealing with callers

Anyone who calls on you uninvited has no right to assume that you want to talk to them, let alone invite them into your house. Keep the back door locked at all times as well. Many tricksters work in pairs and one may keep you talking while the other slips round the back! Don't feel guilty about leaving them on the doorstep while you check their identity. Genuine callers will not object to you taking sensible precautions.

Common confidence tricks include the bogus official who claims to be from the water, gas or electricity company, needing to gain admittance to your home; the doorstep salesman who may try to pressure you into buying expensive products, or persuade you to order some goods and pay a deposit with your order; the workman who claims that there are slates missing from your roof; even the social worker who wants to check on your child.

The official

Once you have checked the identity of the caller through the door viewer, secure the chain or limiter before opening the door. Then ask the caller for some identifi-cation and examine it carefully. Do not rely on the sight of an official-looking uniform. All officials should carry an identification card, so make sure they show it to you.

If you are still in doubt, ask the caller to wait outside and close the door while you telephone the relevant authority. If you are still not satisfied, trust your instincts and ask the caller to come back so that you can arrange for a friend, relative or neighbour to be with you. Phone the local police and let them know what has happened. They may know of tricksters operating in the area, and will certainly look into the matter if they feel your suspicions are justified.

Doorstep salesmen

Many unsolicited callers will be trying to sell goods or a service. People selling expensive home improvement products can make a great deal of commission on sales and may therefore be very keen to persuade you to part with your money, often offering what appear to be very attractive discounts or special terms.

The salesman may offer a large discount if you sign on the spot, or may try to pressure you by saying that prices are about to rise. No matter how persuasive the salesman is, do not be tempted to make a decision there and then. Ask for time to think about the offer. You will often find that the same discount is available if you phone back a few days later.

Also be wary of promises that you can always cancel the deal if you change your mind. You may have cancellation rights, but salesmen know that once they have a signed piece of paper, the chances are that you will go ahead with the purchase. Similarly, do not be swayed by the offer of a generous guarantee.

A simple intercom system, such as Friedland's Password Doorphone, will help you identify the caller and allow you to talk to them without having to open the door.

Do not give the doorstep salesman a deposit for orders placed or goods promised. It is always possible they will not come back with the goods.

The workman

It is easy to be taken in by workmen coming to your door and claiming that there are tiles missing from your roof, or that the guttering is leaking and needs replacing. These tricksters may try to panic you into having the work carried out immediately by telling you that serious damage could occur.

You could find yourself paying an extortionate fee for what may be an unnecessary job, or you may have to pay twice for a professional builder to rectify shoddy workmanship.

Do not accept their claims that work needs doing. If in doubt, get a second opinion from a reputable workman who is personally recommended or who belongs to an association such as the Federation of Master Builders or the Guild of Master Craftsmen. Always get two or three estimates before you agree to have any work carried out.

What the law says

When you buy from a trader who has called at your home without an appointment, you have seven days in which to cancel the contract and reclaim the money you might have paid. This applies to goods you buy and to work you have arranged to have done, provided the sum involved is over £35. This law covers home improvements such as replacement kitchens or double glazing, but not new building work such as home extensions. If in doubt, contact the local Citizens Advice Bureau.

Audio and video entry systems

There are other more sophisticated ways of identifying who is at the door. With an audio or video entry system, you can hear and, with the latter, see your visitors from the safety of your lounge, and even let them in and switch on the hall light – particularly useful if you live in an upstairs apartment or large block of flats, or even a large house.

Audio and video entry systems have become more competitive in price, easier to install and are growing in popularity. They offer convenience, safety and security with the benefit of being able to control who comes in at the touch of a button. There is also the advantage of being able to have a chat with the milkman and the postman without having to run down the stairs in your bathrobe!

Entry systems can be installed in single homes or, using modular components, can be designed to serve as few as two or as many as several hundred residents in blocks of flats or apartments.

While early systems were quite complex and bulky, simpler, more compact systems are now available. The most basic systems use existing bell wire to send both sound and picture from an entry panel incorporating a microphone and a miniature camera, installed at the main door, to a monitor and telephone handset indoors.

What it costs

Cheaper systems may be limited in range, i.e. by the length of the cable over which the system is able to provide good visual and audio communication, but they may be quite adequate for the single home, costing around £500 complete for a video entry system.

Some systems are now relatively inexpensive and can be DIY fitted using just two-wire cabling.

A smart audio-only door entry system with push-buttons for each flat.

Today's stylish monitors blend very easily with your decor. Most can be wall - or table-top mounted.

It is quite possible to use your own TV monitor, running coaxial cable from the outside camera unit via the household aerial and linking in to a spare channel on your set. Many large apartment blocks have a facility built in to do just that, but if you are a resident in a block, please don't go off on your own to tackle the job. You are likely to be encountering higher voltages and a multitude of other control equipment, and only the building maintenance manager or a qualified electrician should carry out the work.

Audio entry kits

With modern technology, the quality and reliability of two-way speech systems has improved immensely. A typical audio-only system consists of an entrance panel with a push-button door bell, for a single home or several apartments, and speaker unit, linked to a telephone handset in the apartment. Normally, a 12v electric release will be part of the kit to convert the door lock to remote control.

Video entry kits

Video entry systems have also improved dramatically, with better and smaller cameras. The video entry door panel incorporates a miniature camera with a lens which is able to adjust automatically to low light levels, so you should be able to see your caller clearly at night as well as during the day.

The monitor/handset indoors will have a number of buttons which allow audio and visual communication. There is usually a time limit on its use – from a few seconds to a few minutes. Just press the button again to restore communication. (Some systems will allow you to view the caller automatically when the door panel button is pushed, using a sensor at the point of entry.)

The depth of the door entry panels, even those incorporating cameras, has been markedly reduced, often less than one brick deep, which reduces the possibility of knocking a hole in your lounge wall. Alternatively, they can be surface mounted.

If recessed, the panel will be supplied with an embedding box. Panels are available in varying materials – anodised metal, aluminium, brass and stainless steel or, if they are likely to be vandalised, you can choose polycarbonate or impact-resistant ABS plastic housings. They can also be fitted with weather-resistant hoods.

Monitors

Monitors can be wall – or table-top mounted (just as a telephone). Wall-mounted screens vary in size – from as large as 18cm (7") to 90mm (3½") flat screen models – and usually provide a black and white picture. They can also be flush or surface - mounted.

The unit is likely to have volume control, remote door release, brightness control, possibly an anti-tamper alarm (alerting the occupier if, for example, someone tries to prise off or damage the outside panel) and a light switch (to provide lighting in a hall or staircase).

There is also a system allowing the camera to 'pan and tilt', which extends the vertical view from 50cm (20") to 91.5cm (36"), and the horizontal view from 66cm (26") to 1.83m (72"). So no-one can lurk undetected.

Power and wiring

Power supplies are usually provided with each kit and can vary considerably, depending on the equipment and its operating range. Obviously, the greater the range, the greater the power needed.

Power will also be needed to operate the electric release which provides remote control of the door. This is usually converted from the supply provided.

Wiring varies considerably, too, from bell wire or six-wire telephone cable to coaxial cable for video con-nection. Most equipment is, however, sold in kits and should be supplied with appropriate connections and, of course, instructions.

Fitting a video entry system

Video entry systems have improved dramatically, with better and smaller cameras. The video entry door panel incorporates a miniature camera with a lens which is able to adjust automatically to low light levels, so you should be able to see your caller clearly at night as well as during the day.

Entry systems have become easier to install and offer convenience, safety and security with the benefit of being able to control who comes in at the touch of a button. There is also the advantage of being able to have a chat with the milkman and the postman without having to run down the stairs in your bathrobe!

Entry systems can be installed in single homes or, using modular components, can be designed to serve as few as two or as many as several hundred apartment residents.

TOOLS AND MATERIALS
☐ Power drill + a range of bits
☐ Mallet
☐ Chisels – various
☐ Hammer
☐ Hiat clips or cabling gun
☐ Spirit level
☐ Trunking
☐ 13amp plug
☐ Screwdrivers
☐ Electrical screwdriver
☐ Tape measure
☐ Pencil

It can be a great advantage not to have to go down several flights of stairs to open a door to a salesman and to be able to release the lock remotely to admit welcome visitors. We fitted our system to a home with living rooms on the first floor.

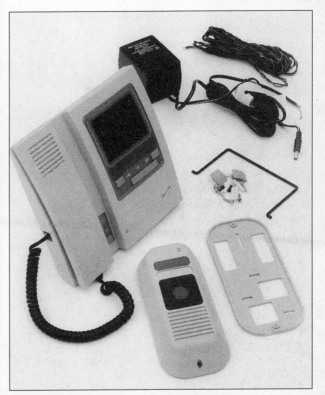

The Vision One video entry system, supplied by BPT, includes a monitor (fitted indoors) and camera unit (which replaces the normal bell push). It also has a power supply unit, mounting plates and two-core wire (you can use existing bell wire if it is in good condition). If you want to fit an electric lock release later you will need to use multi-core cable.

1 The most direct route for the cable was through the landing window. This window frame was very deep and required either a long bit or to be drilled from each side. Either way, drill the frame from the inside first to avoid break-through splinters and re-decoration later. Then estimate the cable length needed outside the house and feed it through the drill hole.

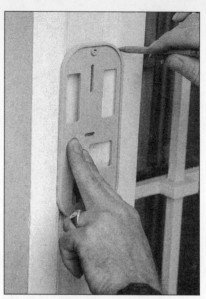

2 Mount the camera unit at about eye level - 1.4m (5'6") above the floor - to allow for the camera angle and average height of people. Avoid placing it where the sun will shine from behind the visitors, as the automatic lens will make their faces dark. Mark the fixing screw positions and the cable entry hole.

3 If the mounting surface is not flat, mark the outline of the plate in order to re-move protruding woodwork. Work round the outline with a chisel, using a narrow one on the curved sections. Remove the wood to a suitable depth with a broad chisel.

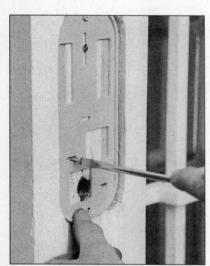

4 If the cable is to be fed through the mounting plate, drill the hole. If not, there is a slot in the plate to accept a cable from below. The existing bell wire hole could be used in this case. Screw the mounting plate to the surface.

5 If you want the cable to enter the unit from the back, you will need to take the cable inside the house and again drill a hole in an inconspicuous place. If you decide to use the cable entry slot in the mounting plate this won't be necessary.

6 Feed the cable through the hole and strip off the insulation about 15 - 20mm (½" - ¾") from the ends of the wire cores. We used eight-core cable and doubled up two of the wires for each connection leaving the other two doubled up connections for a lock release.

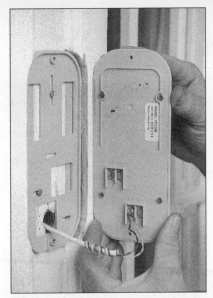

7 Adjustments to the chime and speech volume can be made on the back of the unit before mounting. A switch can be used to stop the internal chime and, if you want to fit a bell to provide a louder warning, connect it to the two extra terminals shown.

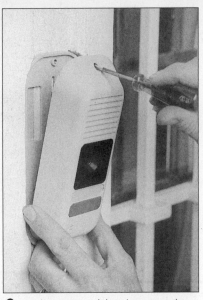

8 Having connected the wires, screw the camera unit to the mounting plate. If a weather seal is not provided, it is wise to apply a smear of silicon grease to the mating surfaces to prevent moisture getting in.

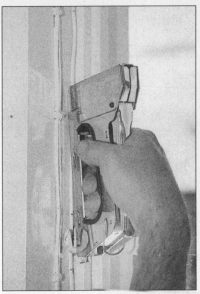

9 Clip the cable neatly into place right back to the monitor unit, leaving a spare length of cable behind the camera unit for servicing. Hiat clips are normally used but a cabling gun makes fixing cable to wood very easy. If fixing around a window, check that the window can open without damaging the cable.

10 If you run cable over brickwork, work with care. You will need to use a hammer and fix the cable run with Hiat clips. If the mortar is hard, you must wear protective goggles.

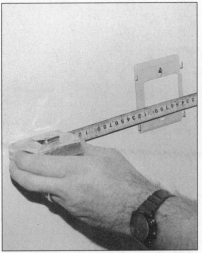

11 Choose a sound wall in a convenient room where the monitor can be firmly fixed, close to a mains outlet. Mark the fixing holes, ensuring the screen can be viewed comfortably by the shortest adult resident. Drill and plug the top hole, then screw the plate for a temporary fixing. Measure, as shown, to ensure a square mounting. Mark, drill and plug the lower screw hole, and secure the mounting plate, making sure it is square and flat.

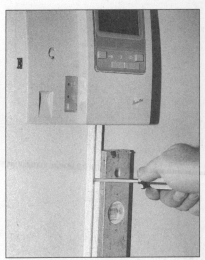

12 To make a neat job of running cables to the monitor, you can chase out the wall and plaster them in. Or you can use trunking. Measure the length and cut it to size. With this model, we cut the top edges at an angle to make the trunking fit the curve of the back of the monitor. Check the vertical with a spirit level, and drill, plug and screw the trunking to the wall.

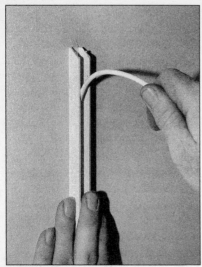

13 Lay the cable in the trunking, and measure for the correct length to the monitor terminals.

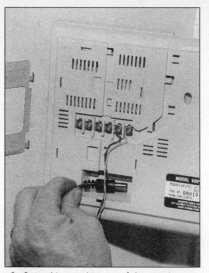

14 Looking at the rear of the monitor, strip the wires back and attach to the two appropriate terminals. The other terminals are for a lock release and an additional speaker. Plug the power supply output cable to the monitor and lay the wires in the moulded grooves to ensure flush fitting. Slide the monitor on to its mounting plate. If you have difficulty, the plate may not be flat or square (see caption 12).

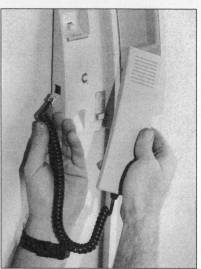

15 Thumb the cables into the trunking. Cut the trunking cover to length, clip it into place and plug the handset into its socket on the monitor.

16 Attach a 13 amp plug to the power cable and plug into the mains outlet. Clip the cable up to the socket and tie up surplus cable. Position the power supply neatly out of the way, ideally using a metal or plastic strap to secure it to the skirting board.

17 Switch the power on and ask someone to call from the front door. Pressing the bar should result in a chime at the camera unit and the monitor.

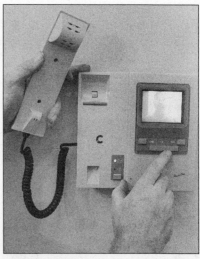

18 The screen powers up for 30 seconds, enabling you to adjust the contrast with the slide bar to suit the lighting conditions. Pick up the handset and talk to the caller to check the system's sound quality. Adjust volume, if required. Press the viewing button and check that the screen stays on for two minutes. This enables the occupant to talk longer or watch the viewing area silently. Hands-free communication is also possible with this model, particularly for a person with limited mobility. Having adjusted the system, make good the drill holes with mastic.

Alarms

Where to start

The extensive range of equipment available can prove very confusing. Your main aim is to find a system which is easy to understand, uses proven technology and can be extended, if necessary, at a later date.

Personal recommendation is probably the best way to choose a company to install your alarm system. However, you may also find your insurance company requires you to use a company that is regulated by NACOSS, the National Approval Council for Security Systems.

NACOSS recognised firms have to install to British Standard 4737 (for wired systems) and comply with the quality assurance standard BS5750. Their systems are regularly inspected and their working procedures must be carried out to the NACOSS code of practice.

There are other associations, including the Security Services Association (SSA) and the Security Group of the Electrical Contractors Association (ECA), whose members are all vetted for suitability and work specifically in the security field. If you check with your insurers, you may well find a company belonging to one of these associations will be perfectly acceptable.

Then, if the installation or system should prove unsatisfactory, you do at least have an official organisation to approach to take up your complaint and investigate the situation.

You should obtain at least three quotes from reputable installers and remember – the cheapest may not necessarily be the best value.

Wired or radio system?

The system offered to you should include a control panel, possibly a remote keypad, detectors (which may include passive infra-red units, magnetic contacts, vibration sensors, ultrasonic sensors or glass-break detectors), a sounder and bell box with a strobe light attached, and personal attack button.

Under the terms of BS4737, the installing company should offer you a maintenance agreement; also, for an annual payment, they may provide a link to a central monitoring station.

The alternative to a wired system is a wire-free radio operated alarm which incorporates all the elements of a wired system but operates over a specially allocated frequency (173.255Mhz). Communication between the main panel, detectors and alarm bell box of traditional alarm systems is normally via special security cabling and powered by the mains electrical supply. Radio, however, means you can install an alarm faster and more easily and you can take it with you if you move.

The system should conform to BS6799, the Code of Practice for Wire-Free Systems. These can be

Some security centres such as Benn Security in Northampton are prepared to put together an alarm kit to suit your home for you to fit. And they give you instructions too!

Linking up to a central monitoring station manned 24 hours a day gives you greater security and peace of mind.

professionally installed or you can buy kits from a range of reputable manufacturers.

You can now obtain virtually any form of detector with a radio alarm, and kits tend to contain a selection with additional units available for you to buy separately as and when you wish to expand the system.

In fact, a good radio alarm manufacturer should be able to supply you with a transmitter capable of adapting any detector for use with a wire-free system. These include magnetic contacts, passive infra-red detectors, glass-break detectors, personal attack buttons and smoke alarms.

You will also have a remote hand-held unit (like those used to operate car alarms) which is used to activate and turn off the alarm.

Terms and conditions

Before you part with your cash or sign a contract, make sure you know whether you are leasing or buying the system outright, whether a maintenance agreement is included in the price and ensure that a 12 month guarantee is offered on parts and labour.

Make sure there are no hidden costs, such as call-out charges or a monitoring service you didn't know about, and find out exactly who is doing the work – whether the company sub-contracts and whether staff are vetted.

Above all, make sure you understand exactly how the system works once it is installed.

The installer should talk you through all the elements of the system and its operation and make sure you can operate it correctly before he leaves. He should also leave you a card or a manual describing the user facilities and the action you need to take.

If you or a member of your family are in any doubt whatsoever make him show you again or explain it more clearly. A very large proportion of false alarms occur simply because the owner doesn't know how the alarm system works.

Doing it yourself

If you do not have to consider insurance company requirements and simply want the peace of mind an efficient alarm system can bring, you may consider installing the alarm system yourself.

There are two ways of approaching this: buy a kit or choose the components yourself. If you buy an alarm in a box from a security centre or one of the major DIY superstores, it should comply with BS6707. Check that it contains both sufficient cable and detectors which will suit your home and protect areas in the right way; also that the overall quality of the components is good.

It is also reassuring to know that the manufacturer provides a 'Help hotline' in case you get into difficulties. Read the instructions very carefully, particularly those relating to wiring, and check that all the listed components are actually there before you begin.

Another way of choosing an alarm system is to visit your local security centre and ask them to make up an alarm kit for you. Not all security centres offer this service but you may be find one that will either issue you with a set of instructions for fitting or be prepared to answer any queries over the telephone.

Unfortunately, neither the police nor an alarm monitoring station will accept emergency calls directly from a DIY alarm system. Nevertheless, you will still have to notify the police that the system has been installed and give them the names and addresses of two keyholders.

Some DIY systems come equipped with an automatic dialling device which, if the alarm is triggered, repeatedly telephones a series of numbers you have chosen until it receives a reply and is able to send a recorded alarm message. Well worth considering if you have elderly or disabled relatives living in the house.

Alarms have improved considerably in recent years and, if used and installed correctly, should give trouble-free and false alarm-free operation.

False alarms have been, and continue to be, a problem and may

Many alarm systems now provide a main control panel and keypads which can be placed in any room from which you can operate the system.

Make sure you know how the alarm is operated before the installer leaves.

sometimes be the reason for home-owners preferring not to install a system or even taking one out if it proves unreliable. It can also attract unwelcome attention from irritated neighbours and disgruntled police.

Control panels

There are no specific British Standards for control panels (or alarm devices themselves), although elements of BS 4737 relate to features found in alarm equipment. This is likely to change with the introduction of European Standards which will, for the first time, require individual components to meet levels of performance and construction.

It is very important to understand how an alarm system is operated if false alarms are to be avoided. To reduce this risk, manufacturers have been making instructions easier to follow and many panels now incorporate a Liquid Crystal Display (LCD) giving plain English step-by-step instructions to guide users through the arming, resetting and disarming procedures.

Precautions to prevent tampering are also built in. The control panel should incorporate an anti-tamper device to deter anyone from trying to prise the lid or attack it in any way. Each zone, the wiring and detectors will also be protected from attack, triggering the alarm if there is any interference with the system.

The control panel will also feature a device to set the alarm and turn it off. This may be a keyswitch (operated by key only) or a keypad, where you will need to use a code (usually four digits) to carry out any procedure.

Most panels allow you to divide your home into zones and set all or part of the system. It will also enable you to set the entry/exit time delay. This is the amount of time you have to enter and turn off the alarm or set the alarm and close the door behind you. It will vary but can be as little as two seconds to over a minute.

Make sure it is set to give you enough time to enter or exit the front door (or your final exit) and disarm/arm the system. The delay will be signalled by a sounder and can instill panic if you have forgotten the code or can't find the key to turn the panel off before the alarm sounds!

The panel will also contain an alarm sounder of its own and should have a 12v rechargeable stand-by battery to take over powering the alarm, for at least eight hours, in case of a power cut. If a primary battery is used as a stand-by, it must be able to run the system for four hours to comply with BS4737. If this runs out, however, it will trigger an alarm condition.

The alarm panel will operate using a 230v mains supply – you should never see a professionally-installed wired alarm panel with a plug attached. It should always be wired in. In addition, alarm panel cabling and existing mains wiring should never be run in the same trunking.

The trend today is to have the control panel hidden away, perhaps in a cupboard, where it is out of sight and not immediately accessible to an intruder. The system will have one or more remote keypads positioned at prominent places around the house which can be used for all the day-to-day programming . Usually not much larger than a light switch, they provide an attractive and discreet system which is relatively easy to operate.

Detectors

The most popular type of detector to protect complete areas – rooms and hallways – is a passive infra-red device (known as a PIR). Also essential to the system are

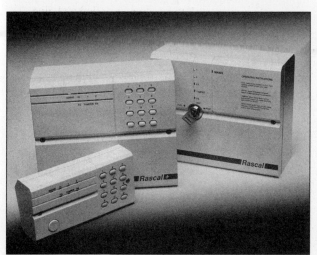

Alarm panel operating options. Choose from a keyswitch, digital code and/or remote keypad.

Everyday operation of an alarm system can be carried out from a neat keypad like this one. An LCD panel gives the user instructions and prompts in simple language.

Alarm components – What goes where

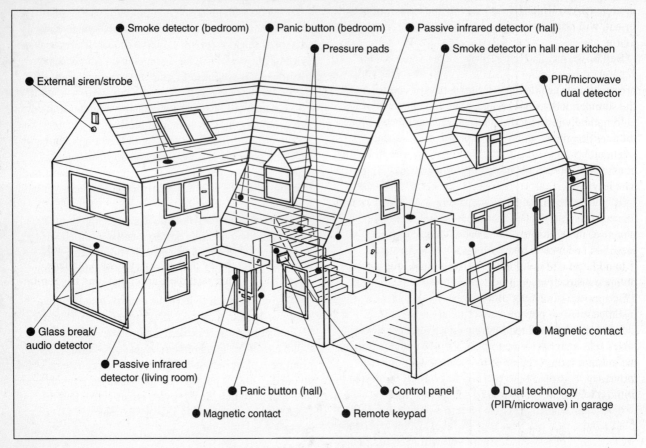

- Smoke detector (bedroom)
- Panic button (bedroom)
- Passive infrared detector (hall)
- Pressure pads
- Smoke detector in hall near kitchen
- External siren/strobe
- PIR/microwave dual detector
- Glass break/audio detector
- Passive infrared detector (living room)
- Panic button (hall)
- Magnetic contact
- Magnetic contact
- Control panel
- Remote keypad
- Dual technology (PIR/microwave) in garage

magnetic contacts (small, flush or surface-mounted devices which protect doors and windows) and one or more personal attack buttons which activate the alarm in an emergency even when it is switched off.

Personal attack buttons usually have a red circular or rectangular push button which triggers the alarm and can only be turned off with a special key.

Other devices used may be ultrasonic or, rarely used alone in domestic situations, microwave. Some detectors now combine two of these technologies, typically PIR plus microwave, in an effort to reduce false alarms, and these are proving very successful in difficult environments.

A very important addition to an alarm system is a smoke alarm. There are smoke detectors which can be wired into an alarm system (the latest Building Regulations specify smoke alarms as a standard requirement in new and newly converted homes) or you can buy a battery-operated smoke alarm, easily fitted.

Monitoring

Most modern panels are able to provide a means of monitoring the alarm. A special device called a digital communicator is installed in the control panel and is able to send a digitally encoded signal, via a normal telephone line, to the central monitoring station.

For an alarm to be acted upon and a message to be passed to the appropriate emergency services (police, fire or medical), the receiving equipment must receive and acknowledge the correct sequence of signals.

Bells and sounders

The bell box can be of polycarbonate or, for high security applications, produced in aluminium and treated steel and powder coated. (BS4737 requires the housing to be of 1.2mm mild steel, 1mm stainless steel, 3mm polycarbonate or equivalent.) Bell boxes should be fixed as high as possible on the house front and may now include a strobe light which will continue to flash after the bell has stopped ringing after the statutory 20 minute maximum period – see over page.

The alarm should also trigger if the bell box is tampered with. This is caused by a self-actuating bell module (SAB) which, if the mains cable is disconnected or cut, will bring in its stand-by battery to sound the alarm.

Bell boxes are also increasingly being fitted with a separate timed cut out (from two to 18 minutes approximately) so that if the SAB takes over operation of the sounder, it does not continue to ring, unless automatically reset by the system, for longer than 20 minutes at a time.

There is a good reason for this. If an alarm is considered to be constituting a statutory offence under The Environmental Protection Act 1990 (Section 80), local authorities have the power to fine the owners of the alarm up to £5,000. The Noise and Nuisance Bill of 1993 increases these powers to enable officers to enter premises under certain conditions.

In addition, the London Local Authorities Act 1991 can oblige owners of offending alarms to fit cut off devices. This applies as much to DIY systems as to professionally installed ones, so beware.

As well as being fitted with anti-tamper devices, bell boxes may also have an anti-foam device which activates the alarm if foam is pumped into the box through the louvres at the side. Some bell boxes are being produced without louvres which also overcomes the problem.

Choosing the right detectors

There are numerous detection devices available and choosing the right one to protect a particular area isn't always easy. There is a whole range of circumstances to take into account – the size of the room, what's in it, even how it is constructed, as well as what's outside or even across the road.

You may need one or more types of detectors in any one area – for example, there are bound to be doors and windows to protect as well as the room itself. There may also be very large areas of glass, such as a patio door, draughts or heating, which may make it difficult to site certain types of detectors, and you may have pets in the house which will mean careful positioning and directing of the detection pattern.

Magnetic contacts

The most basic detection device is a magnetic contact (or reed switch). The reed switch is attached to the fixed section of an opening (i.e. frame of a door or window) and is held in the closed position by a magnet fitted to the moving part. When the magnetic force is removed by the door or window being pushed ajar, the switch opens, cutting off the current (if the alarm is set) and triggering the alarm.

Contacts should be positioned carefully, ideally at the top of the door, with the contact flush mounted in the architrave a few inches in from the catch side of the door. Surface mounted contacts, easier to fit, are often provided with DIY kits. One is sufficient for each opening but it is important they are installed on well fitted and sound frames or you may end up with false alarms.

Detecting shock

Shock sensors come in a variety of forms – inertia, piezo electric and vibration. These are designed specifically to detect force and sounds like splintering wood in the area

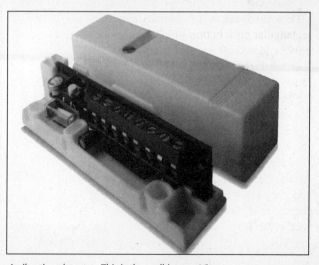

A passive infra-red detector is triggered by a person moving across a fan-shaped pattern of zones.

A vibration detector. This is the well-known Viper.

that is being protected. Once again, it is very important to position these correctly.

Pinpoint the most obvious point of attack, where the intruder may gain access with the least noise; on a window this is likely to be close to the handle where the intruder may try to lever the window open. The sensor should be mounted on the window frame and set at a sensitivity level where it will not trigger the alarm other than when a real attack is detected. You should also check that other sources of vibration, like a nearby road or railway line, will not affect the device.

Independent tests on a correctly fitted vibration sensor showed that it didn't react when the window was tapped, a door knocked or a tennis ball thrown against an adjacent partition. Even a masonry drill used on an external wall about a metre away did not activate the alarm.

Glass break

The problem with glass break detectors is that not all types will work effectively on double-glazing. There are basically two methods. Self adhesive foil strips or tape carrying a current can be applied to the glass. Breaking the tape triggers the alarm (although even a hairline crack can produce this and cause false alarms).

A single strip should be applied no nearer than 30cm (12") to the edge of the glass; the glass is held firmly and any nearer may not shear the foil. If a rectangular pattern, rather than a single strip, is used, then it must be applied no less than 50mm (2") and no more than 10cm (4") in from the edge. It also has to be varnished to insulate it from moisture.

The other method is based on audio (ultrasonic) technology and enables the detector to recognise the particular frequency of breaking glass. Here it is important not to position a detector close to air vents or doors where the noise of glass breaking outside may be picked up, or placed near a telephone.

Laminated glass may also reduce the effectiveness of the device. However, one system is able to measure the flexing effect of a blow on glass as well as the frequency it generates, so glass breaking outside should not create an alarm. These units can also be used to protect several windows at a time, rather than having to fit a device to each window separately.

Panic buttons

A personal or panic attack (PA) button has to be activated deliberately by a person in the house. Usually it's by pressing a hand button, although it is possible to obtain adapted units which can be activated with a knee or foot (often used by retailers, banks and similar premises or by the disabled). The unit activates the alarm via a special 24 hour circuit even when the alarm has not been set and can only be turned off and reset with a special key. PA buttons should be sited as discreetly as possible and are often positioned just inside the front door and by the bed.

Pressure mats

These aren't widely used today but are often included in DIY kits. Available in various sizes, they are suitable for protecting staircases (one may be positioned at the top or

PIRs are getting smaller and more streamlined. This is a Rokonet detector.

A range of dual technology detectors from C+K.

bottom of the stairs), immediately inside patio doors or other possible points of forced entry. Pressure mats incorporate an 'open' circuit which is completed when the intruder steps on the mat. It is necessary to have the underlay of the carpet cut away to avoid the mat showing – an expensive measure if you have to employ a carpet fitter to do it for you.

You should be careful not to place furniture on them by mistake or to install them on uneven floors or on top of carpet tacks or other sharp objects which could pierce the plastic covered mat. They are prone to wear, which could result in a false alarm, and if placed under a thin carpet may eventually show.

Passive infra-reds

The most popular of the movement detectors is the passive infra-red detector (PIR). PIRs look for a change in energy – the infra-red produced by humans – and trigger an alarm if the source of the energy (body heat) moves across a fan-shaped series of zones. In older PIRs, strong sunlight could trigger the detector but most now incorporate a dual sensor system which has zones on two levels so, if the source of heat is static, it should be ignored. Only if the heat source moves across the PIR's range should an alarm be triggered.

PIRs are supplied in a choice of ranges – long, wide, corridor and curtain – and can cover as little as 3m (10') up to as much as 40m (about 133'). The long and corridor lenses have fewer zones across a narrow width but can detect movement as far as 30 or 40m away. The curtain type is suitable for protecting doors or windows and particularly large areas of glass. The pattern is a vertical one running parallel with the area to be protected and creates a solid protected zone. These are also useful if the house is open plan with a mezzanine floor for the bedrooms. The pattern would be able to detect anyone jumping off the mezzanine or a break-in through the ceiling from a loft.

Pet alley patterns allow an area at ground level for pets to walk around safely without triggering the alarm. However, this means that an intruder crawling by would not be detected and it also doesn't prevent pets jumping on to furniture and setting off the alarm. The only way really to avoid this risk is to keep dogs and cats, and any other warm-blooded animals likely to roam, confined to

one room where a movement detector is not in use. A room protected by contacts or shock detectors would also be secure from pet false alarms.

Some PIR detector manufacturers now supply masks with a standard scanning unit which enables the coverage pattern to be modified to prevent the PIR from seeing 'hot spots'. You can adapt them to different circumstances rather than having to buy completely different units.

PIRs are susceptible to moisture – ensure that those used to control exterior lighting, for example, are IP rated. This is a grading system which shows the level of resistance to dirt and moisture; they should be at least IP44 to IP55. Insects, too, can cause havoc if they get into the casing or even walk across the sensor if the optics aren't sealed. PIRs should also be resistant to radio frequency interference (RFI).

Ultrasonic and microwave

An ultrasonic is an active, rather than a passive, detector. This type of detector is particularly useful in a glass conservatory or perhaps to protect an indoor swimming pool, as the energy it transmits is easily contained within a small area; a PIR is susceptible to sun and headlights penetrating the glass and may cause false alarms in these circumstances.

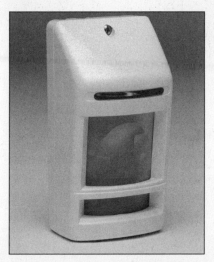

A passive infra-red detector suitable for domestic situations, the Apollo from Guardall.

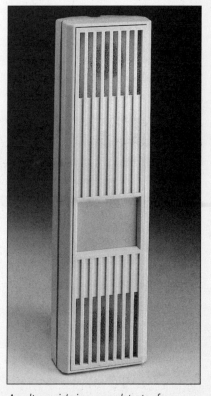

An ultrasonic/microwave detector from Aritech.

The device generates a low frequency (about 20KHz) and incorporates a receiver and transmitter allowing it to compare the received energy with the original transmitted frequency. Stationary objects, such as furniture, will return the same frequency but, if an intruder is moving within the area, a changed frequency will be returned (known as the Doppler effect) and an alarm signalled.

Once prone to false alarms, a new method of signal processing incorporated in ultrasonics has reduced the problem and they can be effective if used correctly. However, draughts or the effects of air conditioning equipment can affect ultrasonics.

Similarly, microwave alone has limited domestic uses, particularly in homes where its capacity to cover large areas is not widely used. It also has the disadvantage of using radio waves which can penetrate glass and brick and even water running down a plastic drain pipe could activate the alarm. They can be particularly tricky to site and should really only be installed by an expert.

Dual detectors

A fairly recent advance is the combination of microwave (or ultrasonic) and PIR technology in one detector. If, for example, you have a detector (perhaps a PIR) which is persistently false alarming because of the surroundings, a dual detector may well solve it. A number of manufacturers now produce these and, although more costly than a single technology unit, they have been very effective in reducing false alarms as each technology is able to 'talk' to the other, checking that both sensors have detected an alarm condition before actually triggering the alarm.

Sounding the alarm

There are several ways to alert others to an emergency, whether it's a burglary, someone in trouble, a medical crisis or even a fire.

The obvious way is to have an alarm sounder outside the house and a flashing light to indicate an emergency. The light will continue to alert passers-by after the statutory 20 minutes during which the siren is allowed to sound.

However, if you are in an isolated situation, with few passers-by, a lot of noise may not bring help fast enough. Or maybe you feel people are so used to hearing alarms that they tend to ignore them. As an alternative or addition to a bells-only system, it is possible to sound the alarm silently. This has the added advantage of keeping the burglar in the dark as he will be unaware that he has triggered the alarm.

Monitoring stations

If you have a modern alarm system, the control panel can easily be linked to a central monitoring station. This usually involves a special device fitted in the control panel called a digital communicator, which in turn can automatically 'pick up' your BT telephone line and send a digitally coded message indicating the emergency (intruder, medical or fire) to the receiver at the monitoring station. This enables staff who are on duty 24 hours a day to call the appropriate emergency service and get them to you as fast as possible. The alarm is triggered in exactly the same way as an audible system – by detectors, panic buttons or smoke alarms.

One thing to remember about digital communicators is that they 'dial' the telephone number of the monitoring station. Inevitably problems may arise when telephone numbers change (such as the BT code changes in April 1995). This means that, if you have a digital communicator fitted, your alarm installer will have to reprogramme it.

This should not entail a special (costly) visit but could be done at the six-monthly maintenance check, necessary for any system with remote monitoring facilities. Don't be misled by stations who claim that the use of 0891 or similar 'chat-line' type numbers avoids this problem – they could, in fact, cost you more. However, Linkline 0345 or 0800 numbers do not incur extra cost.

To fit a digital communicator, the equipment and initial connection can cost from £100 up to £250. You will also need two maintenance visits a year from the alarm company (around £60) and there will be an annual monitoring fee of around £65 to £75. With Telecom Red

A central station offers 24-hour monitoring for your alarm system. It can receive alarm calls via a digital communicator installed in your alarm panel, Telecom Red CARE or Paknet signalling systems.

CARE (see below), there is a further monitoring fee from the BT network of some £110 a year. You will also need BT to fit a block terminal, which involves an engineer call-out and costs around £63 plus VAT.

High risk areas

While the digital communicator is the most popular way to connect homes to a monitoring station, they may be vulnerable in higher risk areas. If the telephone line is cut or tampered with, the alarm signal will not get through.

To overcome this problem, there is an alternative system offered by BT called Telecom Red CARE. This service continuously monitors the existing telephone line and, if the line is put out of action, there is an alternative secure route for the signal to follow, a parallel network which duplicates the signalling.

There is no need to have a second telephone line – all the user is aware of is a small box (a Subscriber Terminal Unit) linked to the alarm panel.

One further advance is the use of radio to signal alarm conditions to monitoring stations. Typically, a radio pad fitted with an anti-tamper switch and a concealed aerial is fitted in your home, and the system automatically tunes into the best of 14 frequencies to send the signal. No telephone lines are involved, the whole system can be set up very quickly and an alarm is received within seconds.

If you do decide to have your alarm monitored by a central station, ensure that your system is installed to BS4737; that the station complies with and operates under BS5979; and that you have two keyholders with telephones available who can respond to an alarm if you are not there within 20 minutes.

In an emergency it is reassuring to know that your alarm will bring help.

Although personal attack alarms are immediately passed by the central station to the police, other types of alarm have to be verified by the station by a telephone call to the user before they are passed to the police (as would be in the case if there were some indication of duress, no reply or some other cause for suspicion).

The alarm then has to be reset by an engineer, although an increasing number of control panels enable the system to be reset from the central station. This would happen, for instance, in the event of a false alarm when the system itself was not faulty or requiring repair.

If you have persistent false alarms (over six in any 12 months) police response can be withdrawn, except for personal attacks. Response is usually restored after three months if no further false alarms occur.

Looking after the elderly

For those who are concerned about elderly relatives living on their own, there are a number of devices, linked to the telephone, which will automatically dial several numbers until they receive a reply and can send a pre-recorded message.

One, resembling an alarm panel, will signal intruder, fire or personal attack and communicate with up to four pre-programmed telephone numbers – including, perhaps, a car phone or an office. The numbers can be changed whenever necessary and you can record and change your own message.

Another emergency telephone dialler will dial up to six telephone numbers if triggered by a hand-held radio transmitter. The recipient has to make a return call to ensure further dialling stops, a feature which overcomes the problem of emergency calls getting through to an answering machine.

Sheltered accommodation

If you have relatives living in sheltered accommodation, where there is no warden-controlled alarm system, it is still possible to have a similar system installed, even without a normal intruder alarm at the premises.

These systems use a special telephone which incorporates a microphone for two-way hands-free speech. They can automatically dial pre-programmed phone numbers and allow the user to answer the phone without having to get up. They can also be fitted with smoke and PIR detectors, which are wire-free, communicating with the main console by radio.

In the mid-1980s, the Department of Trade and Industry issued the special radio frequency of 173.225MHz on which alarm systems could operate. Most radio alarms use this frequency, although there are some exceptions. Products which haven't been approved for operation in these frequencies are illegal. Approved equipment will carry a label with an identifying number.

You should also check with your insurance company before installing a wire-free system in preference to a wired system. They may insist on a wired system if the risk is high or they have specifically asked you to install an alarm.

The range of a radio alarm should easily cover a typical house – about 90m (300') in 'free air space' is often quoted. However, certain things may reduce the range of the signal – low-power, walls and steel-girders, for example, may prevent a signal getting through. Other things to watch for are metal water pipes and mains cables, and you should avoid mounting the control unit close to computers or fax machines.

It is a good idea to do a 'walk-test' before finally positioning the sensors. Most systems will allow you to check that the system works effectively before finalising it. Look out for 'dead' spots. These can be overcome by moving the transmitting unit a few centimetres.

The control panel will have to be plugged in (kits usually provide a transformer for this purpose) or wired into the mains, with a stand-by 12v battery which will maintain the system if there is a power cut. (Systems complying with BS6799 must not use a plug and socket for connection to the mains.)

Setting the house code

The usual practice is for a house code to be set which will be repeated throughout the system where a transmitter is incorporated with a detector. This is usually achieved quite simply with a series of small switches in each unit; some systems will also allow you to set a zone code, so each detector or group of detectors can be allocated to a different zone, enabling you to identify quickly which has alarmed.

The system may have several zones allowing you to part-alarm the house. It should also have a variable entry/exit setting to give you enough time to enter and exit before the alarm is triggered. Detectors should also trigger a low-battery warning light at the control panel - it is important to change the batteries regularly according to the life-expectancy suggested by the manufacturers.

When you are setting the code in the detectors, make sure that the control panel is switched off, as the detector will have an anti-tamper device fitted and will therefore trigger the alarm when you remove the housing!

Wire-free alarms can easily be extended. A workshop, shed or garage could be brought into the system by simply fitting a detector and setting the same house code (preferably a magnetic contact rather than a PIR as these

can be susceptible to changes in heat levels or bright lights). And security lighting can also be brought into the system with the use of external radio-operated PIRs used to trigger existing lamps.

Professional alarm installations offer a number of benefits. The installation should be neat and tidy, with wires tucked away out of sight. The work involved should cause little inconvenience and upheaval and, provided the installer shows you how to operate the alarm correctly, you should not have problems with false alarms. But professional installations can be expensive and, if cost is prohibitive, a competent DIY enthusiast with knowledge of wiring and electrical work, should be able to install a fairly comprehensive DIY intruder alarm in a weekend.

With DIY alarms, you can either buy a kit from DIY multiples or security specialists, or you can visit the latter for advice and purchase individual components to make up an alarm system that will exactly meet your specific requirements.

Depending on how much you pay, a standard DIY kit may include only the absolute basics for perimeter protection, such as a simple control panel, bell box, magnetic contacts for doors and windows, and possibly a panic button. It may not offer devices to detect movement inside the home.

By buying components individually you can achieve a much more sophisticated DIY system which, for example, incorporates a superior control panel offering a number of zones, passive infra-red detectors to sense movement, and vibration detectors. Obviously price will determine the final system – but the result should be a professional alarm system without the installation costs.

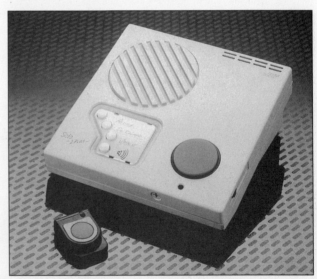

Systems that use an automatic dialling system triggered by a panic button or pendant to alert a central monitoring station or warden control centre are ideal for the elderly or infirm.

So, where do you start? First you will need to draw a floor plan showing both upstairs and downstairs, and all windows and doors. Think about your particular requirements. If you live in a flat or bungalow, you may only require what is known as a single zone system, with windows and doors protected, and a panic button by the bed.

If the property has an upstairs you will probably require at least two zones which can be controlled independently. This would enable you to secure the downstairs only, when the family is asleep at night, or would allow you to alarm all the external doors and windows, whilst disarming interior protection devices when you are at home during the day.

Think also about other family members; if there are children in the house you may want a control panel that is particularly easy to operate. Or, if there are pets, you will not want a PIR guarding areas where they have free access when the alarm is set.

The number of zones which your control panel offers will, to a large extent, govern the level of protection which your system provides. If, for example, you want to install several passive infra-red detectors to protect a number of rooms, each will require a separate zone. The installation sequence at the end of this chapter uses a six-zone panel for greater flexibility and ease of installation.

A security centre may be prepared to offer advice, based on your floor plan, and show you a range of alarm components from different manufacturers. If you choose to install a DIY kit, it should conform to BS6707, the British Standard for Intruder Alarm Systems for Consumer Installation. A BS6707 approved alarm should have an audible alarm which will cut out after 20 minutes; failure to limit the amount of noise emitted by an alarm system can lead to prosecution for noise nuisance.

If your alarm is made up of individual components, it will not conform to BS6707, as this is only for complete systems. Components, however, should conform to BS4737; in which case you should not come across problems with component compatibility when installing your system. You should not attempt to start installing a system until you have ascertained the components you require, and the siting of each.

There are a number of points to bear in mind when considering siting to reduce the risk of false alarms:
● Make sure that the distance between the control unit and your exit door can be covered easily in the time delay between setting the alarm and the system becoming operational.
● Keep the control panel accessible but out of reach of young children.
● Make sure doors and windows fit securely and do not rattle or vibrate in response to high winds or heavy traffic.
● If there is a 'nightset' zone, such as leaving the upper floor unarmed for night-time convenience, make sure the family know where they can and cannot go, and banish pets from armed areas.

The ideal mains supply for an intruder alarm system is direct from the consumer unit, on its own fused spur. This can be prepared before beginning the installation but must not be connected until installation is complete. The control should not be wired into a lighting circuit or a

Often professionally installed and complying with Class III of BS6799, Scantronic's 4600 system has a main control panel, and a choice of passive infra-red detectors, magnetic contacts, vibration sensors, panic buttons, remote set/unset unit and smoke detectors.

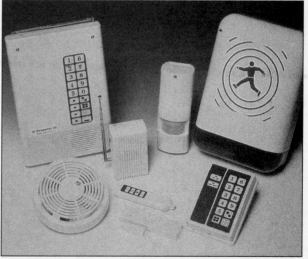

The Response RE3000, designed for DIY installation, can be expanded from this basic kit to cover more than one zone.

ring mains into which appliances with electric motors are plugged. Motors generate mains surges which can cause the microprocessor to malfunction momentarily. If in any doubt about the installation, contact a competent electrician.

Installation

Once you have decided on the position of each detection device, you need to plan the route of the cables from the devices and the external sounder to the control panel. DIY kits are often supplied with cable, mounting screws, wall plugs and cable clips but, by buying extra cable, you can achieve a more professional installation, running concealed cables the long way round rather than having short, visible cables which will make your alarm installation look amateur.

Easily concealed under carpets, cables should be run alongside gripper rods to protect them from being crushed. Alternatively, there may be a gap under the skirting board, wide enough to accept the cable. They can also be run under floorboards or buried in the wall but test the circuit before covering the cables.

For ground floor movement sensors, cable can be dropped down from the first floor. Visible cable should be concealed with plastic trunking or secured with clips at frequent intervals (about every 15cm or 6").

The control panel should be firmly fixed to the wall with the mains supply taken, if possible, directly from the consumer fuse box and via a 2 amp fused spur. Door contacts can be fitted anywhere along the opening edge of the door or on the top of the door within 15cm (6") of the opening edge. Always use a surface mounted contact on the final exit door.

Passive infra-red detectors should be fitted to a flat surface in the top corner of a room, in a position where they will deter intruders and protect a likely point of entry. They must not be sited over a heat source, nor looking directly at a window, and the alarm cable must not be run near mains cables.

Do not use PIRs where large air movements are likely, such as a garage, or where warm air heating is in use. Each PIR must be connected to its own zone, with no other devices on that zone. Personal attack buttons should be sited near the front door, and/or in a bedroom, and out of the reach of small children. If there is more than one personal attack button on the circuit, they should be wired in series.

The sounder enclosure, or bell box, should be fitted in a prominent position where it cannot easily be tampered

Wire-free alarm systems are particularly easy to install.

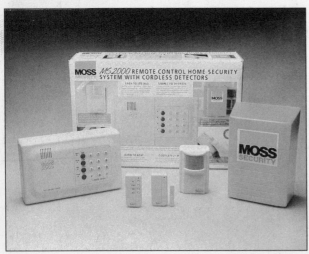

A Moss Security kit which is widely available and reasonably priced.

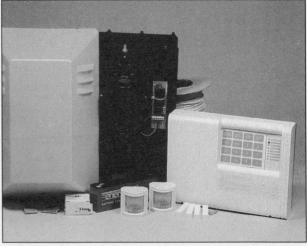

With DIY alarms you can either buy a kit like the expandable AJ600 from A1 Security, or you can purchase individual components to make up a system.

with. Its visibility can be extremely effective in deterring intruders. The bell box should contain a self-actuating bell which will power the sounder in the event of its disconnection from the control panel. The connecting cable from the sounder should be taken through the wall directly behind the enclosure and run to the control panel.

Instructions for your DIY system or control panel should take you through testing of the complete system during and after installation. This will ensure that components are installed and operating correctly and will minimise the risk of false alarms.

Once the installation is operational, make sure each member of the family knows how to use it. Appoint two keyholders who will be able to see to your system should an alarm condition occur while you are out. They must know how to operate and silence the alarm. Notify the local police station that you have installed an alarm and give them the names and addresses of the keyholders so they can be contacted in an emergency.

For greater security, you may be able to link your alarm to a communicator. This provides low-cost 24-hour monitoring of your alarm system. In the event of an alarm situation, it sends programmed alert messages to up to four contact telephone numbers selected and programmed by the user.

Stand-alone systems

The term DIY alarms can also encompass simple battery-operated or plug-in devices which require little in the way of installation skills.

Battery or mains-operated stand-alone devices can be used to protect one room, to detect intrusion through a door or window or positioned in a hall to protect several rooms. These devices normally incorporate a passive infra-red detector to sense movement and, in response, trigger a loud built-in sounder which can operate as a deterrent.

These alarms are no substitute for a comprehensive, built-in system but do offer benefits in the fact that they may be moved around from room to room. They are ideal for protecting garages, greenhouses, sheds, workshops, caravans, boats – even protection for personal belongings in hotel rooms, with prices ranging from £20 up to about £100.

Other simple DIY systems are designed to operate via the ring mains; components are simply plugged into 13 amp sockets around the home via adaptors. They detect break-ins by sensing changes in air pressure caused when doors or windows are opened or broken. The devices can

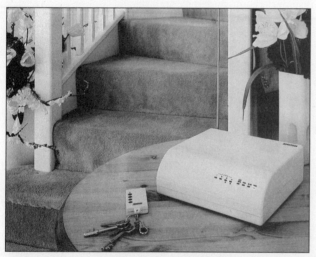

Smiths Wireless control unit can be table-top or wall-mounted.

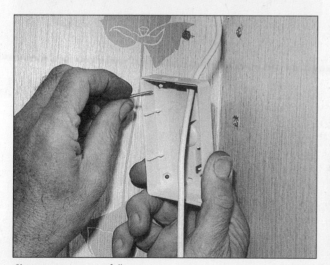

Site components carefully.

Locate the control panel as close to the mains supply as possible.

also be linked to an external sounder for greater protection and can be expanded to protect outbuildings via the addition of magnetic contacts, patio door contacts or passive infra-red detectors.

A comprehensive system comprises a master alarm unit, slave unit and two infra-red movement sensors to provide coverage for at least two points of entry in the home. Each unit plugs into a 13 amp socket and they 'communicate' via the regular mains wiring. The system is easily expanded with a range of additional detectors and an external siren and strobe. Depending on the electrical conditions, security can be shared with a neighbour via this system. By installing a slave unit and alarm enhancer in the neighbour's home they will be alerted should someone break into your home, and vice versa.

The final option for a comprehensive DIY system is the wire-free alarm which uses radio transmission between detectors and the control unit. Although many of these are designed for professional installation, there are kits available specifically for the DIY market. Wire-free systems will probably work out slightly more expensive than a wired DIY installation.

Whilst a DIY installation will undoubtedly save you money, it will be a false economy if the installation is faulty and continually causes false alarms. Not only will it upset your neighbours but, at the end of the day, you will probably stop using it altogether, leaving your home vulnerable.

Make sure that, if you attempt an installation, you have the knowledge to carry it out effectively. Bear in mind also that a DIY installation is very unlikely to qualify you for a discount on your house contents insurance. This is normally restricted to installations carried out by an installer recommended by your insurer, or one who is NACOSS or police-approved.

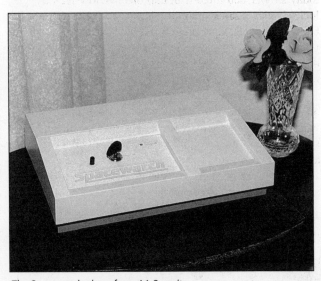

The single unit SAS02 from Smiths Industries is an installation-free, air-activated alarm system which detects break-ins by sensing changes in air pressure caused when doors or windows are opened or broken.

The Spacewatch alarm from A1 Security.

Safes

Nowadays, there is a strong case for keeping jewellery, valuable documents, computer disks, sentimental items and cash out of sight and out of reach in a safe. Once you have made this decision, it is important to bear in mind a number of points.

Depending on the type of safe you choose, you could fit one in a cellar or the attic, both places a thief may not care to venture in case he is trapped. Free-standing safes can sometimes be fitted in a wardrobe or cupboard or under the stairs – you could even disguise one as a window seat or a television stand! – and underfloor safes should, ideally, have furniture placed over them.

However hefty it looks, an old safe is often far from effective, constructed in materials easily beaten by today's tools, and fitted with unprotected, low security locks. Today's safes are built with specially developed barrier materials, layer upon layer, with the highest grades able to resist oxyacetylene torches. The locks are designed to be more difficult to pick and are usually reinforced with steel plates.

That doesn't mean it isn't possible to buy a good quality second-hand safe but make sure it isn't pre-1945, which would be virtually useless. Some locksmiths who specialise in safes re-condition them and, if you buy from a reputable company, such as a member of the Master Locksmiths Association, you can be sure that both safe and lock will be up to standard.

Safes can be free-standing and bolted to the floor, underfloor and sunk in concrete, flush fitted in brick walls, concealed under floorboards and fitted between joists, or simply be steel containers which are disguised to resemble other items – an electric socket or even a can of hair spray!

There are also fire safes and cabinets which, although fine for protecting valuable documents from damage in a fire, should not automatically be considered secure or able to resist forceful attacks. Likewise a safe built for security is not necessarily resistant to fire.

A free-standing safe can be bolted to the floor of a wardrobe. This is a Chubb Heritage.

An underfloor safe, conveniently concealed, is ideal for securing family heirlooms and jewellery.

A range of wall safes from Churchill. It's surprising how much they will hold, but check cash ratings carefully.

Fire safes are built of several layers of material designed to spread the heat. Their resistance is usually measured in hours, something you should look for if you wish to store material such as computer disks or tapes (known as media safes). They come in various forms, from a simple document safe resembling a cash box to a hanging file unit or free-standing unit which can be bolted to the floor.

There are basically two types of safe. Those providing a high security and resistance to determined attacks, and those which rely on disguise and are intended to conceal items of lower value – which, if discovered, would probably offer little resistance.

Most domestic safes, except the low security hide-away types, are able to resist cutting, drilling or grinding tools – sledge hammers, chisels, drills or angle grinders, for example.

If you are fitting a safe because your insurance company says so, then you should establish what level of insurance rating is necessary. Two figures will be given - the cash rating and jewellery rating - and you will find most safe manufacturers are able to quote these in relation to particular models. A cash rating of £3,000, for example, will provide a jewellery rating of £30,000. Before buying the safe, make sure your insurance company is happy with your choice.

An underfloor safe is considered the most secure and there is a wide range of sizes available. Smaller units can be used for cash, passports, credit cards, jewellery and other items, while the larger models are capable of holding boxes of jewellery, cameras, ornaments, stamp collections and hand guns. (We cover gun cabinets and the requirements for guns later on.)

Features to look out for, apart from the insurance rating and level of security or fire protection, are: the number of bolts; that the interior is lined with felt or velvet to protect jewellery or ornaments from damage and to prevent condensation (not just to look pretty!); and that the safe

Two types of novelty hide-away safes, the Strongpoint and Vent-Safe, from Ashley Security Products.

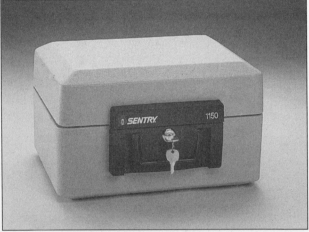

If you want to avoid this happening to important documents, use a proper fire-resistant cash box like this one from Sentry who offer a wide range of fire safes and files, some of which are also suitable for computer software.

has at least a seven-lever lock which retains the key if it isn't actually locked (so you cannot walk away with the key if you forget to lock it).

If you tend to mislay keys, a combination lock may be the answer, or even an electronic digital lock, although this will inevitably add to the cost of the safe. Also look out for safes that have a re-locking mechanism which jams the bolts in the locked position if the safe is attacked.

Underfloor safes

You can choose a square door safe or a round door. Some round door safes have a deposit tube which allows cash to be inserted without lifting the entire door. These are often used by retailers who prefer not to hand the safe keys to their staff.

A point to watch is that the people using the safe are strong enough to lift the heavy door to open it. A gas-pump – (also referred to as a strut) assisted door makes it much easier to lift out and there are many models, often with interchangeable doors, with different types of lock, number of bolts etc., and a choice in body sizes so you can choose one that gives the appropriate features. Other models offer a hinged door but this may limit access.

Free-standing safes

The advantage of a free-standing safe, other than its accessibility, is that it is possible to take it with you if you move. They come in sizes from 60cm (2') square right up to bank vault size. However, don't presume larger sizes are necessarily more secure.

There are several ways of installing free-standing safes but most important is to ensure that the floor on which it stands will be able to support its weight. Don't forget it also has to be transported to its final place, so make sure your floor will also take the weight of the delivery men (say 125kg, about 19st, per person!) – you may need to reinforce a suspended timber floor.

Anchoring is usually through the base of the safe. The most popular method of fixing the safe to a concrete floor is with an expanding steel sleeve which is inserted into a hole drilled in the concrete, fixed with a steel bolt, and then passed through the base of the safe and screwed into the expanding sleeve. There may be one or two of these fixing points.

If the floor is wooden, a special fixing anchor with a rubber expansion sleeve moulded over a threaded insert is placed in the hole. The safe is positioned on top and then the base fix bolt is inserted through the safe into the

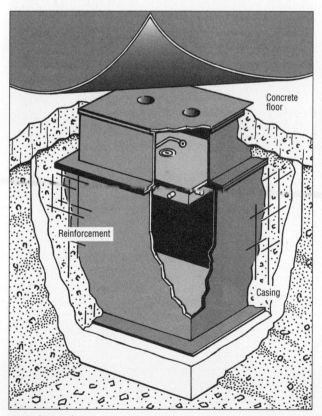

Underfloor safe

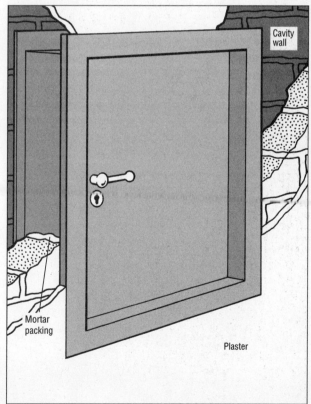

Wall safe

sleeve and tightened, expanding the sleeve to form a strong anchor. Alternatively a base fix plate may be used in conjunction with countersunk screws. The plate has a threaded boss which aligns with the safe base fix hole.

Wall-safes are designed in brick sizes – two, three or four (see picture sequence on p.66) and will hold an amount of small items, such as jewellery, documents and cash. They, too, may have an insurance rating, so check this with your supplier. Expect to pay from £85 to £130 depending on size – more for one with a combination lock and a shelf.

Alternatively you could fit a 'floorboard' safe, especially designed for DIY and fitted between the joists of any suspended floor. These are relatively easy to fit and make a good, fairly secure hiding place.

You will need to remove sections of the floorboard to expose the joists (look for the rows of nails on the floorboards to locate the joists). There should be a distance of 40.5cm (16") between the centre points of the joists – if not, you will need to nail or screw a piece of timber to them to make the gap measure 35.5cm (14").

Then, having marked the area, use chisel out 3mm (⅛") of the timber from the top of the joists for the flanges of the safe – some models don't require this and are built to match the standard floorboard thickness. This allows the box to drop flush so that the top of the safe is level with the top of the joists; it also allows the floorboards to fit flush with the surrounding floor.

Then mark the positions of the four coach screws through the holes provided in the safe walls. Remove the box and drill the four starter holes – no less than 6mm (¼") diameter and no more than 25mm (1") deep. Replace the box and secure it in position with the coach screws provided. Various sizes are available and the smallest will cost from around £70 or £80.

'Above floor' safes, suitable for DIY installation, start from around £189 for a 25cm high by 25cm wide model (10" x 10"), fitted with a seven-lever lock or a combination lock and constructed to satisfy most insurance companies (depending on the risk).

Always keep weapons and ammunition in a safe place. Gun cabinets should comply with the Firearms (Amendment) Act 1988.

Gun cabinets

The Firearms (Amendment) Act 1988 requires shotgun certificate holders to keep their guns securely in a locked gun cabinet or similar secure container. Prior to the Act, over 700 shotguns were reported stolen annually and could easily have fallen into the wrong hands.

Gun safes come in various sizes and can accommodate several guns; larger units containing a lockable compartment for ammunition. Usually of 2mm to 3mm (about ⅛") continuously welded steel, they should also have two high security locks (at least seven levers) reinforced with steel plates, be resistant to jemmy attacks and other forceful measures, and have protected hinges, preferably concealed.

They will need to be anchored to the wall and should be pre-drilled to enable easy fitting. If coach bolts are difficult to fit – they would show on the other side of the wall – use 10mm x 80mm screw bolts (⅜" x 3¼") and self-tap their thread into soft brick or blockwork, once an 8mm (⅓") pilot hole has been made.

Some manufacturers produce disguised gun cabinets which can be built into furniture or are ready-made to look like a tallboy or chest of drawers.

Simple DIY

Often the simple ideas are the most effective and, depending on the level of security you require, there are some neat, cost-effective ideas which effectively conceal cash and jewellery, particularly if you are travelling. For example, one manufacturer produces a range of look-alike cans of household products. The top or bottom of the cans twist off to reveal a storage area, but look and weigh just like a full can of, say, household cleaner or polish.

Other companies produce safes which look like an air vent and an electrical socket (see pictures on p.62). Both have a six lever lock and conceal a steel box which makes up a drawer section. They are designed to be fitted between courses of brickwork or in standard cavity walls and are easily installed.

Look-alike cans offer a convenient hiding place

Fitting a wall safe

Ideally, a safe should be hidden but not obviously so – such as fitting a wall safe behind a picture. It can be hidden behind window curtains, for example, but no closer than 25cm (10") to the edge of the opening where the window fits (i.e. the reveal). It should also be positioned where limited space would make it difficult to attack – with the swing of a sledge hammer, for example.

Wall safes, available in brick sizes, are not difficult to fit but remember, the size of the safe is restricted by the thickness of the walls. A solid wall must be at least 23cm (9") thick, or it may be fitted in a 28cm (11") cavity wall. Often, the only walls thick enough are outside walls. Building or breeze blocks do not provide secure mounting points.

TOOLS AND MATERIALS

- [ ] Power drill
- [ ] Long masonry drill
- [ ] Hammer
- [ ] Bolster chisel
- [ ] Gloves
- [ ] Spirit level
- [ ] Sand
- [ ] Cement
- [ ] Grano
- [ ] Pencil

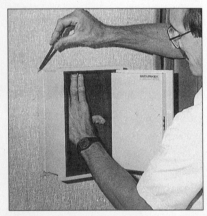

1 Making sure there are no wires running where the safe is to be installed, mark the required position of the safe with a pen or pencil.

2 Next, drill a small hole through the wall. This will indicate whether or not the wall is of sufficient thickness for the installation of the safe.

3 The hole in the wall must be 25mm (1") bigger on all sides than the actual safe. Drill a hole in each corner and use a hammer and chisel to remove the plaster.

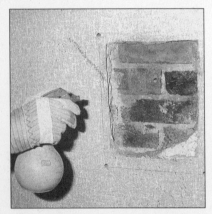

4 A tip from the experts – spraying the opening with plenty of water keeps dust down to a minimum.

5 Use a drill to weaken the bricks so they can be removed more easily. An alternative method is to drill rows of holes all the way round so the block falls out more or less in one piece.

6 Take care to ensure that rubble does not fall down the cavity as this can lead to problems with damp. Line the cavity with newspaper to prevent this.

7 Remove as much dust as possible and wet the wall thoroughly to ensure that the mortar will stick.

8 Check the fit of the safe and then mix up some sharp sand, cement and grano (one part cement to three parts sand and grano) to secure it. Grano is available from builders merchants and will make the mortar much harder.

9 Lay a neat pile of mortar at the bottom of the hole and place the safe on top with a wedge positioned underneath. Use a piece of wood or a spirit level to make sure it is straight.

10 Tape up the side of the safe to protect the hinges and cement it in place, pushing the mortar well back.

11 For a smooth finish cut back the mortar and cover it with a layer of plaster or smooth cement.

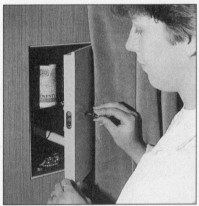

12 With installation complete, our Securikey wall safe in four-brick size provides ample room for the safekeeping of passports, legal documents and items of jewellery.

Fitting an underfloor safe

Today's safes are built with specially developed barrier materials, with the highest grades able to resist oxyacetylene torches. The locks are designed to be difficult to pick and are usually reinforced with steel plates.

Most domestic safes are able to resist sledge hammers, chisels, drills or angle grinders. An underfloor safe, sunk in concrete, is considered the most secure and, ideally, should have furniture placed over it to disguise its whereabouts.

Check the number of bolts, that the interior is lined with felt or velvet and that the safe has at least a seven-lever lock. A gas-pump (or strut-assisted) door is much easier to lift out. Models come with interchangeable doors, different types of lock, number of bolts and choice of body sizes.

TOOLS AND MATERIALS

☐ Demolition hammer
☐ Lump hammer
☐ Bolster chisel
☐ Gloves
☐ Spirit level
☐ Concrete
☐ Polythene sheeting
☐ Liquid lino paint
☐ Paint brush
☐ Polystyrene fibres

1 Fitting an underfloor safe involves burying it in concrete, reinforced with steel mesh or metal reinforcement rods. Depending on the type of floor you have, this can be a messy business. If you already have a concrete floor, you will need to drill a hole at least 15cm (6") larger and 7.5cm (3") deeper than the safe, using a 'demolition' hammer.

2 Layers of concrete are then built up around the safe, compacting each layer (each about 7.5cm or 3" deep) with a 25mm (1") square steel rod. The concrete mixture must be allowed to cure for seven days in a damp atmosphere and, to prevent rapid drying, it should be covered with polythene sheeting, sealed around the edges. Once dry, it is advisable to paint the surface with a liquid lino paint to stabilise it and reduce the risk of dirt and grit entering the safe mechanism. The reinforcement grid shown here, supplied by Hamber Safes, is ideal for a home handyman's installation.

3 While the safe is being installed, the safe door should be placed well away from the site to avoid any form of contamination. After the safe and grid have been lowered on to the level concrete base of the hole, further layers of concrete, well mixed with polystyrene fibres, are stamped down into position. Fill the safe itself up to the neck with crumpled newspaper to protect the interior. The final 10mm (¼") or so of screed should be a mixture of sharp sand and cement in a 4:1 ratio. When the installation is complete, no portion of the neck or deposit tube should protrude above floor level.

Security marking

Property marking is a worthwhile and inexpensive security measure, which offers two major benefits. Marked property is more difficult to dispose of and can, therefore, deter a thief. And, if the worst should happen, your possessions stand a better chance of being returned to you if they are recovered by the police.

Up and down the country police are inundated with recovered stolen goods which cannot be returned to their rightful owners simply because there is no means of identifying them. Police always check recovered property both for visible identifying marks and, with an ultra-violet lamp, for invisible marking. If an identifying code is found, the police can decipher it and return the property to its rightful owner.

The recommended method of security marking is to use your postcode, which narrows your location down to a specific geographic location, followed by the number or first two letters of your house name. For instance, if you lived at 7 New Road, Anytown AN14 3BR, you would mark your property with AN14 3BR 7. If you lived at 'Beechwood', New Road, Anytown AN14 3BR, your code would be AN14 3BR BE.

If you are not sure of your postcode, your local Post Office will be able to tell you; or check in your Thomson Local Directory.

If you move house, don't try removing the old code. Simply put an 'X' by the side of it and then mark your possessions with the new postcode. This allows the police to trace the history of ownership if necessary.

If you rent a home, or move home frequently, using your postcode may not be appropriate. In such cases, there are companies who offer computerised marking services by subscription. Each subscriber is normally allocated a personal code number which is stored on a computer with the subscriber's name and address and other necessary details for police reference.

The company supplies marking stencils and materials to enable you to mark your property. Should your property be recovered, police will note your code number and check it via the computer. Computer marking companies are best sourced via your local police station to find a reputable firm.

Marking methods

There are various methods of marking property. You will probably need to adopt several in order to mark a variety of surfaces. Many police stations have property marking kits, which you can borrow, or a Neighbourhood Watch scheme or Residents' Association may like to get together and buy a kit to be shared by members.

Police also frequently organise bicycle coding days, when you can have your bicycle die-stamped. Property marking pens are also readily and cheaply available from security centres, DIY superstores, department stores and newsagents. On most surfaces, the best form of marking to use is visible marking. There are various methods including etching, die-stamping, branding, identification paint and indelible ink.

Die-stamping is best used for large metal objects, such as bicycles, lawnmowers and tools. Even if a thief files down the mark, it can usually still be detected by forensic tests. Similarly, identification paint can be used on bulky objects where appearance doesn't matter.

Police always check recovered property for visible identifying marks. An ultra-violet lamp is used to detect invisible marking.

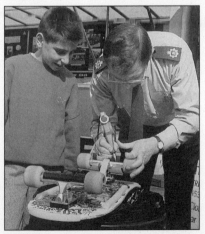

Local police often organise cycle coding and property marking events when you can take items along for marking.

Etching leaves a permanent mark on hard surfaces. Use a stencil to achieve a neat finish.

Etching is ideal for hard surfaces, such as televisions, video recorders, cameras or hi-fi equipment. There are two methods. The first requires the use of a hard-tipped engraving pen, usually supplied with a stencil to help you obtain a neat, legible mark. The second method is acid-etching, or sandblasting, which is carried out professionally to apply vehicle registration numbers to car windows.

Ceramic markers may also be used to mark hard surfaces such as glass, porcelain or china. However, unlike engraving pens, ceramic markers do not scratch into the surface but deposit a permanent metal compound. Again, these are easy to use and usually supplied with a stencil. To apply a mark, keep the area moist. If the tip of the marker begins to blunt, it can be sharpened with a carborundum stone available from hardware stores.

Invisible ink

When the concept of security marking was first introduced, the most popular method was 'invisible' marking, which utilises ultra-violet fluid, normally contained in a pen for ease of use. This can only be detected under ultra-violet light.

Whilst still a good marking method for specific surfaces, uv marking does have disadvantages. A uv mark is not permanent – exposed to natural or artificial light, the mark will fade over a period of time. It is important, therefore, to check the mark every six months and reapply it as necessary.

All the same, it is a useful means of marking clothing, leather goods and other objects which you do not wish to deface - always test the pen on a hidden area first as the ink may lightly etch some surfaces or be visible in direct sunlight on non-porous surfaces. Also, remember to reapply the mark each time an item of clothing is cleaned.

Antiques or other items of considerable value should not be marked without obtaining expert advice first in case it reduces the value.

Once you have marked your possessions, it's worth advertising the fact! Most property marking pens are supplied with 'Warning – Marked Property' stickers to put in your window; alternatively they may be available from the Crime Prevention Officer at your local police station.

Small items

Some articles are too small to write your postcode on but jewellery is a popular target and often difficult to describe when it goes missing. The best way to improve its chances of being returned is to keep a visual record of each item.

You can either take photographs or use a video camera to record items on tape. Each one should be logged in colour against a plain background and next to a ruler to give an idea of scale. Keep a written record of any distinguishing marks or features such as hallmarks, crests, initials and even cracks, chips or dents.

Written records

Keep a written record of all your property, along with serial numbers and, for insurance purposes, values (it's always a good idea to keep receipts for this purpose). Make a copy of the list and leave this and your photo negatives or duplicate video tape with a relative, neighbour or solicitor, just in case you lose the originals.

If you're ever faced with a room full of recovered, stolen property and are trying to identify your own possessions, you'll be pleased that you took the trouble to make your mark.

Sandblasting is carried out professionally to apply the registration number to car windows and headlamps.

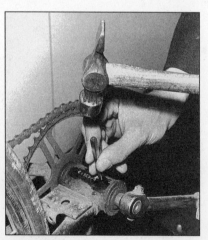
Die-stamping is best used for large metal objects, including bicycles, lawnmowers and tools.

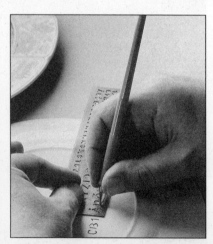
Ceramic markers deposit a permanent metal compound – ideal for marking glass, porcelain or china.

SECURITY MARKING
WATCHPOINTS

1	**Security marking** helps to ensure that lost or stolen property may be **safely returned**.
2	Use your **postcode** and **house number**, or first two letters of its name, to provide a **unique code**.
3	To invalidate a code, put an **'X'** by it and write the new code.
4	**Look out for security marking days organised by the police**.
5	**Don't forget tools** in the garage and/or shed.
6	Remember to **check and reapply** ultra-violet marks where necessary.
7	**Never mark antiques** without expert advice.
8	Display **'Marked Property' stickers** in your windows.
9	Keep a **visual record of small items**, with identifying marks.
10	**Keep written records, with serial numbers and receipts**.

Remember to display 'Marked Property' stickers in your windows to deter would-be thieves.

Property check list

ITEM	MAKE	MODEL	SERIAL NUMBER
Television 1			
Television 2			
Video			
Hi-fi			
Home Computer			
Printer			
Typewriter			
Camera equipment			
Camcorder			
Clock			
Antiques			
Other valuables			
Fridge			
Freezer			
Microwave			
Washing machine			
Tumble drier			
Dishwasher			
Food processor			
Bicycle 1			
Bicycle 2			
Power tools			
Lawnmower			

Use these pages to record all your security marked property, and keep them in a safe place. List jewellery separately with hallmarks, distinguishing marks and features, together with a photographic record.

VALUE	WHERE MARKED	PHOTOGRAPHIC RECORD
£		Yes ☐ No ☐
£		Yes ☐ No ☐
£		Yes ☐ No ☐
£		Yes ☐ No ☐
£		Yes ☐ No ☐
£		Yes ☐ No ☐
£		Yes ☐ No ☐
£		Yes ☐ No ☐
£		Yes ☐ No ☐
£		Yes ☐ No ☐
£		Yes ☐ No ☐
£		Yes ☐ No ☐
£		Yes ☐ No ☐
£		Yes ☐ No ☐
£		Yes ☐ No ☐
£		Yes ☐ No ☐
£		Yes ☐ No ☐
£		Yes ☐ No ☐
£		Yes ☐ No ☐
£		Yes ☐ No ☐
£		Yes ☐ No ☐
£		Yes ☐ No ☐
£		Yes ☐ No ☐
£		Yes ☐ No ☐
£		Yes ☐ No ☐
£		Yes ☐ No ☐
£		Yes ☐ No ☐
£		Yes ☐ No ☐
£		Yes ☐ No ☐
£		Yes ☐ No ☐
£		Yes ☐ No ☐
£		Yes ☐ No ☐
£		Yes ☐ No ☐
£		Yes ☐ No ☐
£		Yes ☐ No ☐

Fighting fire

Each year in the UK there are over 50,000 accidental fires in the home and many people are injured. An early warning and a contingency plan for what to do in the event of fire are important considerations which could do much to reduce damage and, more important still, prevent injury or death.

Kitchen hazards

Cooking appliances are the most frequent cause of accidental fires in the home. Care should be taken with saucepans on the cooker, particularly if there are young children at home, and handles should be positioned so that they don't overhang a hot ring or burner, or the edge of the stove. Never lean over the hob when it is switched on and make sure that tea towels do not overhang the cooker.

Chip pan fires are a particular hazard. Once switched on, chip pans should never be left unattended. Never fill a pan more than one-third full with fat or oil and do not insert wet chips. When you have finished cooking, turn off the heat and remove the pan from the heat source.

If a fire does start, do not attempt to move the pan. Turn off the heat, if it is safe to do so, cover the pan with a lid or damp cloth and leave to cool for at least half an hour. If you cannot control the fire, shut the door and call the fire brigade immediately. Safer than a chip pan is a thermostatically controlled fryer which can be purchased from most electrical stores.

Smoking

Many deaths and injuries result from carelessly discarded cigarettes and matches. Lighted cigarettes or pipes should never be left lying around; they could easily fall on to upholstery and start a fire.

Always make sure you have plenty of deep ash trays around and check upholstery for cigarette ends before going out or to bed. Empty ashtrays last thing at night – preferably into metal bins with lids – and make sure they are properly extinguished. Never smoke in bed – dozing off while smoking a cigarette or pipe could cost you your life. Finally, make sure matches and lighters are kept out of the reach of children.

Electric appliances

Fires caused by electrical faults, accidents or misuse of electrical equipment are very common. Maintenance of house wiring and appliances is vital for safety. Wiring should be checked regularly. If your home still uses round pin plugs, or if the wiring is over 25 years old, it probably requires replacing.

Indications that wiring is dangerous include plugs and sockets that are hot to the touch, and fuses which blow for no apparent reason. Wiring should be checked by your local electricity company or by an electrician on the roll of the National Inspection Council for Electrical Installation Contracting (NICEIC).

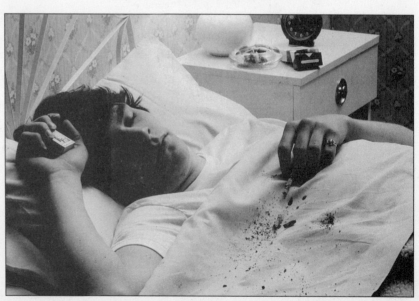

Cooking appliances are the most frequent cause of accidental fires in the home.

Never smoke in bed – dozing off while smoking a cigarette or pipe could cost you your life.

Appliances should be checked regularly and frayed flexes replaced. Flexes should never run near hot surfaces or under carpets, where they could be damaged without being noticed. Always use the correct fuse for equipment. Make sure that your home has enough electrical sockets to avoid having to use multi-way adaptors and wires trailing across the floor.

When joining flex, use purpose-made connectors – never twist the wires together. Never cover light bulbs with fabric or paper; always switch off electrical appliances when not in use, and remove plugs from sockets. If you suspect that an appliance is faulty, do not use it until it has been properly checked. Never attempt any electrical jobs unless you know exactly what you are doing.

Electric blankets can be very dangerous when misused. They should be kept dry and flat and should be serviced every two or three years (you can ask the shop you bought it from to arrange this for you). Buy a blanket which conforms to British Standard BS3456, preferably one that has over-heat protection. An electric underblanket should always be switched off before getting into bed. Some overblankets are designed to be left on but check the manufacturer's instructions.

A portable heater should be kept well away from inflammable materials and areas where it could be knocked over, or where something is likely to fall on it.

Heaters

Chimneys should be swept at least twice a year if you burn ordinary coal, once a year if you use smokeless fuel. If you think the chimney is on fire, call the fire brigade immediately and remove any materials that could catch fire. Always put a fire guard in front of the fireplace, using a British Standard approved all-enclosed guard, particularly if there are children or elderly people at home. Remember to damp down the fire before going out or off to bed.

Portable heaters should be kept well away from flammable materials and areas where they could be knocked over or where something is likely to fall on them. Do not use portable heaters to dry clothes.

Gas appliances

When lighting a gas cooker or heater, you should always be ready to light the burner before you turn on the gas. If you have an appliance with a pilot light, it should light immediately. If it doesn't, turn off the gas and check that the pilot is alight.

If you smell gas, extinguish cigarettes and never use matches or a naked flame. Do not operate electrical switches. Open doors and windows and then check to see whether a tap has been left on or a pilot light has gone out. If you suspect a gas leak, turn off the main gas tap (usually located next to the gas meter) and call the gas company immediately.

Gas appliances should be serviced regularly and should be installed by British Gas or by a member of CORGI.

Bottled gas should always be stored in an outbuilding, never in the home, and must be protected from heat and frost. Cylinders should be changed outdoors or in a well-ventilated room. If you suspect a leak, test by brushing soapy water over the joints and connections. If bubbles appear, the cylinder is leaking and should be capped and placed outdoors until it can be checked by an engineer.

Night-time safety

Many serious fires are those which start at night, taking hold before they can be discovered. It is crucial therefore to have a bedtime routine.

Before retiring to bed, switch off all electrical appliances (except those designed to be left on) and remove plugs from sockets. Empty ash trays, making sure that their contents are extinguished and discarded safely, and check furniture for cigarettes and matches. Damp open fires down. Finally close all doors so that, if a fire does break out, it is less likely to spread quickly to other parts of the house.

Smoke detectors

Should a fire break out, your chances of survival will be much greater if a smoke alarm is installed. By providing the earliest possible warning, this gives you a vital extra few minutes to escape.

The growing use of smoke alarms in the home has not only reduced the number of deaths in fires (now the lowest figure since 1971) but also increased the number of fires detected early on, before they take hold. Domestic fires where smoke detectors have given early warning have risen by 164% since 1988.

Nevertheless, 75% of deaths in fires are in the home and most of these are caused by the misuse of cooking appliances. Half are started in the kitchen, while a third are caused by smoking and smokers' materials.

Choosing a smoke detector

If you don't have a smoke detector, now is the time to fit one. There are several types on the market, ranging in price from under £10 to over £20. Models use either ionisation or photoelectric detection and can be mains or battery-powered. Make sure they conform to BS5446 Part 1, 1990 and display a British Standard kitemark, as this shows they have been adequately tested. Ionisation units contain a tiny amount of harmless radioactive material (said to be less radioactive than a house brick) and can detect tiny changes in an electric current flowing in the chamber caused by smoke particles in the air. They are able to respond quickly to flaming fires.

Photoelectric alarms use pulsating light beams which 'see' smoke and are claimed to respond more quickly to smouldering fires.

Mains-powered alarms

Recent legislation means that new and newly-converted homes must be fitted with mains-powered smoke detectors. Although long familiar to professional alarm installers and electricians, they are now becoming more generally available. These alarms must be interconnected and can be powered by either mains electricity, mains electricity with battery back-up or low voltage via a mains transformer.

Battery-operated models, using a 9v battery, are perfectly acceptable for existing homes, however, and these are available from most DIY and hardware stores and security specialists. They are very simple to fit with just a battery to insert and two screws to secure the unit to the ceiling. Be careful where you fit the device, however, as ionisation units are sensitive and may trigger if you burn the toast or the oven smokes while grilling chops, for example.

Smoke detectors are saving lives every day by detecting fires at an early stage.

Choose a smoke detector with a BS kitemark.

Where to fit a smoke alarm

Ideally, fit one alarm on each floor of your home but, if you are only fitting one, make sure it is between the sleeping and living rooms – the lounge or kitchen.

A smoke alarm should be fitted on the ceiling in the centre of a room or a hallway. If you have to fit the alarm on a wall, it should be around 15cm (6") from the ceiling so it can detect smoke as it rises. If the room has a gable, the alarm should be fitted about three feet from the highest point. If you can, fit a detector at the top of the stairs and inside or outside each bedroom.

Don't fit a smoke detector in the garage, where exhaust fumes could set off the alarm or insects could get into the unit, or in bathrooms and kitchens where condensation or cooking fumes could affect it. Battery-operated detectors don't usually work in extreme temperatures – below 4°C (40°F) or above 38°C (100°F) – so don't fit them in a conservatory, boiler room or cold store room.

If fitting a detector at the top of the stairs makes testing the unit or changing the battery difficult or dangerous, find another spot, or choose a unit which can either be tested by shining a torch beam across the test button or has an extra large button which can be pressed using a broom handle or walking stick.

You would still have to reach it to change the battery, of course, something you should do at least once a year, although the unit will give a low battery warning. Make sure you always have a spare battery – fire chiefs have pointed out that while many people have fitted smoke detectors, quite a large percentage are not in operation because the owner has not bothered to change the battery. A long-life alkaline battery can last up to three years.

Special features

Some detectors are fitted with a light which comes on automatically when the alarm is triggered. This is designed to help you make your escape in smoky conditions and if there is a power failure. Others are fitted with a 'pause' button, which allows you to silence the alarm and reduce its sensitivity for around eight minutes – so you can finish burning the toast!

These are suitable for caravans or similar confined areas. The alarm should automatically reset after the stated time. Some smoke alarms can be interlinked so that if one is set off, others elsewhere in the house are triggered at the same time.

Recent developments include a portable detector (not intended to replace permanent devices) and a smoke alarm designed to fit in place of a ceiling rose. It can be fitted directly into the existing house lighting circuit without the need for additional wiring and without interfering with the normal light switch operation. The switch can, however, be used to test the alarm and provide a 'pause' facility. Rechargeable, stand-by lithium batteries provide at least a ten year life.

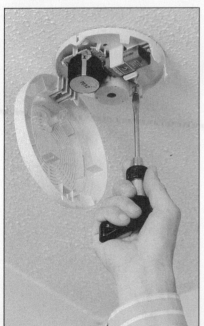

Fitting a smoke detector is very simple. Fit the battery, and screw the unit to the ceiling. A ratchet screwdriver can be handy here.

A smoke detector should have a test button. Sometimes these can be operated using a torch so you don't have to climb on a chair or steps.

You can now buy smoke detectors which can be interconnected so that if one is triggered the others elsewhere will alert people in other parts of the house.

Extinguishing the flames

You should always have at least one fire extinguisher handy around the house but choose the right type and learn how to use it properly. Halon gas is now banned because of its ozone depleting affects and other alternatives are being developed. Powder, foam, water and CO_2 gas cover most eventualities, with powder the most suitable for the home.

A fire blanket is very useful in the kitchen, particularly for smothering chip pan fires, still one of the largest causes of fires. They can also be wrapped around a person to smother the flames. Usually wall-mounted, made of woven glass fibre and with quick release tabs, they should conform to BS6575: 1985.

Making an escape

If a fire does take hold, you will need to get yourself and your family out of the house as quickly as possible. It can take less than 60 seconds for a small fire to fill your home with highly poisonous smoke and fumes. It's a good idea, therefore, to plan an escape route in advance. Try to plan two escape routes from each room and make sure that all windows and doors can be opened easily. Keep a torch handy to use during your escape and keep keys to hand to allow a prompt exit.

If a fire does break out, close the door of the affected room to delay the spread of fire and smoke. If closed doors feel warm, do not open them, as you will release the fire. Get everyone out of the house and do not go back in to save possessions.

Phone the fire brigade from a neighbour's home or from a phone box. Warn neighbours if your home adjoins others. If you are cut off by the fire, try to get everyone into a room at the front of the house; close the door and use bedding or other materials to seal any gaps. Go to the window and try to attract attention. If the room begins to fill with smoke, stay as close to the ground as you can.

If the fire is so severe that you must escape before the fire brigade arrives, climb out through the window, breaking the glass if it is jammed. Remove jagged glass and cover the lower sill with a blanket. Drop bedding or cushions on to the ground to break your fall and climb out, feet first, lowering yourself to the full length of your arms before dropping. This should only be attempted from first floor windows.

If you live in a flat, never use the lifts in the event of fire – always use the main or escape staircases.

If clothing catches fire, lie down immediately and roll across the floor. If someone else's clothing is alight, force them to the floor and wrap a blanket, rug or carpet round them. Call medical help as soon as possible.

One other fire safety device worth considering is an escape ladder. Make sure the ladder has stable brackets which fit inside the window, a spacer which keeps you away from the building as you climb down and has strong enough rungs, preferably of heat-resistant, non-corrosive steel. Some units can be stored in a cabinet in a room where exit is most likely, or be folded away beneath the window. Typical prices range from £45 to £70.

It can take less than 60 seconds for a small fire to fill your home with highly poisonous smoke and fumes.

An emergency escape ladder like this one from Eliza Tinsley could help you make a safe exit.

FIRE SAFETY
WATCHPOINTS

1 Keep **portable heaters** away from anything combustible.

2 Do not place a **clothes horse** near a **fire or the cooker**.

3 **Always** stub out cigarettes in a deep ashtray.

4 **Never** smoke in bed.

5 Surround heaters and fires with a **large guard**.

6 Do not stand **portable heaters** where they can be knocked over.

7 Do not use a **candle** or **naked flame for lighting**.

8 Store **inflammable liquids** in a cool, safe place (out of sunlight), in **clearly labelled containers**.

9 Make sure **loft insulation** is **non-combustible**.

10 Buy **flame retardant nightwear** and **bedding**.

11 Make sure **upholstered furniture** conforms to safety standards.

12 Buy a **fire blanket** and a suitable **fire extinguisher**.

13 Fit a **smoke detector** which has a **BSI kitemark** and conforms to **BS5446** Part 1 1990.

14 A newly built house or a newly converted home must be fitted with **mains-powered smoke alarms**.

15 **Change the battery in your smoke alarm regularly**.

16 **Test** smoke alarms **every month**.

17 **Once a year,** remove the cover and dust or vacuum the inside of the smoke alarm to ensure insects are not trapped.

Chubb do special dual packs of a fire blanket and fire extinguisher for use in the home.

Which Extinguisher to Use

Class of fire	Water	Spray foam	CO₂ Gas	Powder
Type A Paper, Wood, Textile & Fabric	■	■		■
Type B Inflammable liquids		■	■	■
Type C Inflammable gases			■	■
Electrical hazards			■	■
Vehicle protection		■		■

Insurance

Figures from the Association of British Insurers (ABI) indicate that three million homeowners may be under-insured and, in the event of a claim, would not have sufficient cover to compensate for stolen or damaged goods.

If you are not insured, you would be well advised to get in touch with an insurance company or broker immediately. Most policies cover your home contents for theft, fire, lightning, escape of water from tanks or pipes, oil leaking from fixed heating systems, storm, flood, subsidence, falling trees or aerials, riot or malicious acts, explosion, earthquake and impact by aircraft, vehicles or animals.

The home contents policy will normally cover your furniture, furnishings, household goods, kitchen equipment and other appliances, food and drink, televisions, videos, computers and audio equipment, clothing, personal effects and valuables such as jewellery and personal money up to stated limits.

It should include accidental breakage of mirrors, glass tops on furniture and fixed glass in furniture, and it may also include accidental damage to televisions, videos, home computers and audio equipment, with cover for accidental damage to all contents available as an extension to the standard contents cover.

Most policies also offer extensions such as a contribution for alternative accommodation should your home be so badly damaged that it is not fit to live in, and for various legal liabilities.

Remember that a standard home contents insurance will not cover every eventuality or risk, and only limited cover applies to contents temporarily removed from the home, such as jewellery or cameras. Cover for such items is often available, as a special extension of home contents insurance, as 'All risks' insurance. To find out exactly what your policy offers, and whether cover is adequate, make sure you read it thoroughly and, if in doubt, contact the insurance company who will be able to advise you.

Choosing a policy

Rates for the same cover can vary greatly, so it does pay to shop around. An increasing number of companies are now offering discounts to householders who have installed good locks to doors and windows or who have a professionally-installed intruder alarm system. (In high-risk areas, this may be a requirement before insurance is even granted and will not qualify for a discount.)

Also check your policy regarding the situation in the event of a claim; those who get a discount for security measures must use the locks or alarm. The policies may not pay out if the alarm is not activated or windows unlocked overnight or when the home is unoccupied.

Other insurance companies offer discounts to members of Neighbourhood Watch schemes, or to householders over a certain age on the understanding that the home will be occupied most of the day; and some are now offering no-claims discounts or loyalty bonuses for those who remain with the same insurance company each year.

You can also save money by offering to pay a voluntary excess, i.e. you agree to pay the first part of any claim up to a pre-set limit. You may find that your policy imposes a compulsory excess of, say, £50, but you can sometimes offer to pay more to reduce the premium.

Also check the minimum sum each policy will insure for. You may find that you actually require less cover, so shop around for a policy which offers a lower minimum.

Basically, home contents insurance can be broken down into two main types – 'indemnity' and 'replacement-as-new'. If you insure on a 'replacement-as-new' basis, you will be paid the full cost of repairing damaged articles or the cost of replacing them with equivalent new articles if they are stolen or destroyed. With 'indemnity' insurance, you will be paid the cost of repairing damaged articles or replacing what has been stolen or destroyed, less an amount for wear and tear and depreciation.

Insurance cover check list

	Lounge	Dining room	Kitchen	Hall/stairs	Lof
Carpets, rugs & floor coverings					
Furniture: tables, chairs, stools, settees, cabinets, sideboards, bookcases					
Bedroom, bathroom & kitchen furniture					
Soft furnishings, curtains & their fittings, cushions					
Televisions, videos and audio equipment					
Household appliances: cooker, fridge/freezer, washing machine, tumble drier vacuum cleaner, electrical goods, heaters					
Cooking utensils, cutlery, china, glass, food, drink					
Valuables: gold & silver articles, jewellery, furs, pictures, clocks, watches, cameras, ornaments, collections					
Sports equipment, books, cycles, CDs, records, tapes, computers, toys, musical instruments					
Garden furniture, lawnmower, ladders, tools, paint, fuel					
Household linen: table linen, towels, bedding					
Clothing					
Other items					

If your policy is not index-linked, add on a suitable allowance for inflation. You may, of course, have other rooms and possessions not listed here.

ding	1st bedroom	2nd Bedroom	3rd bedroom	Bathroom	Garage/shed	TOTALS

TOTAL **£**

Allowance for inflation during year at %

Your contents should be insured for **£**

So, in the event of a claim, the money you get back from the insurance company will only be enough to buy second-hand furniture or new furniture of inferior quality. You will normally find that items such as clothing and household linen can only be insured on an indemnity basis.

Sum insured

The sum insured is the amount of money for which your home contents are covered. In the event of a claim, it is the most your insurers will pay, so it is vital that you calculate it accurately but, at the same time, you do not want to pay for cover that you do not need.

When you are assessing your sum insured it is easy to miss items. The most effective method is to study every room, including the loft, garage, shed and any other outbuildings and estimate how much it would cost to replace each item at today's prices (visit the shops if necessary to gain a comparison).

You will also be responsible for rented items such as televisions and videos, so do not disregard them. Remember to deduct an amount for wear and tear and depreciation of clothing and linen. The ABI recommends that this is calculated on the following basis: a suit is estimated to have a life span of five years, so for every year, deduct ⅕th of the price of an equivalent new suit at today's prices. This is only a rough guide – allowances will be made for the quality of the suit and its general condition.

For valuables and antiques, an expert valuation may be required. There is usually a limit on the value of any one work of art, ornament or piece of jewellery and often an overall limit on such articles. Keep valuations and receipts secure, as they may be required if you make a claim.

As you add up the total value for each room, write it down on the ABI checklist printed here. When it is complete, add up the figures you have entered in the boxes and write in the total.

To ensure that the figure remains up-to-date, many policies are index-linked, i.e. your sum insured is automatically changed every month in line with the government's Retail Prices Index. If index-linking applies, the total is the sum insured you need. If your policy is not index-linked, you will need to add a suitable allowance for inflation in the year to come.

It is very important that the sum insured is adequate and you must remember to ask your insurer to increase your sum insured if you add to your possessions. Some policies state that, if you are under-insured, claim payments will be reduced. Even if the policy is index-linked, the sum insured should be reviewed every few years.

Buildings insurance

As well as the structure itself, a buildings insurance policy will cover the permanent fixtures and fittings, such as sanitary ware and fitted kitchens, and interior decoration. Policies usually extend to cover out-buildings such as garages, greenhouses and sheds, and limited cover is provided for boundary walls, fences, gates, paths, drives and swimming pools.

Most policies cover damage to your home caused by a variety of risks, including fire, lightning, storm and flood, theft or attempted theft, subsidence or landslip (with an excess applying in almost all policies), explosion or earthquake, malicious damage or vandalism, riot, damage from leaking pipes, escape of oil, and impact by vehicle or animal.

Among the usual extensions are the cost of alternative accommodation up to a certain limit; property owner's liability; accidental damage to underground service pipes and cables; and breakage of glass in doors, windows and skylights and sanitary ware.

The amount a building should be insured for is based on how much it would cost to rebuild it completely and, again, the sum insured must be adequate as it is the most your insurer will pay under any circumstances.

Most policies specify that the amount to be paid, even for less serious damage, can be reduced if there is under-insurance. Advice on how much to insure your home for is available in the 'Buildings Insurance for Home Owners' leaflet available from the ABI. This gives details of the costs of rebuilding according to the type, size, age and location of the house.

Buildings insurance is normally offered by mortgage lenders when you buy your home but it pays to shop around, as this may not be the cheapest or most suitable policy available.

If your home is at high risk from subsidence, it is worth remaining with the same insurer as some won't pay if the damage was caused before you were insured by them. Ideally, policies should be index-linked so the cover is increased in line with the House Rebuilding Costs Index produced by the Royal Institute of Chartered Surveyors. You will also need to increase the amount you are insured for if you carry out substantial home improvements.

Making a claim

Before you contact your insurance company, make sure that the type of damage you are claiming for is covered, and check whether you should claim under your buildings or contents policy. Then contact your insurance company, building society, broker, agent or adviser and request a claim form. This should be completed and returned as soon as possible, ideally with estimates for repairs or replacement.

If you are the victim of theft, malicious damage or vandalism, inform the police immediately and, if cheque books, credit cards or cash cards have been stolen, notify the issuing company, bank or building society.

If temporary repairs need to be made to prevent further damage or intrusion, arrange for them to be carried out straight away. Keep the bills, as the cost may form part of your claim. Keep damaged items, as the insurance company may need to see them.

Once your insurance company receives the completed claim form, they will request estimates for repair work or replacement, if not already submitted. They may then pay your claim; arrange for their claims inspector to call on you; or send a loss adjuster to handle the claim.

The loss adjuster will advise you on any matter relating to your claim and inform you if the insurance company requires further information. They will also agree claim settlement figures with you. If you do not have purchase receipts and professional valuations for any item lost or stolen, ask the insurers what alternative evidence they will accept.

If you are unhappy with the way a claim is handled, write to the insurance company branch manager to say so. If you are still not satisfied, contact the head office. If the difficulty remains unresolved, contact the Association of British Insurers Consumer Information Department. Most companies subscribe to schemes which provide for an impartial body to consider complaints if you have been unable to reach an agreement with your own insurance company.

INSURANCE WATCH POINTS

1 Shop around for **discounts** and **adequate cover**.

2 **Read the policy carefully**, paying particular attention to advice on claims and conditions.

3 **Keep your property in good order**. A policy does not cover the costs of maintaining your house or its contents.

4 You must take **reasonable steps** to prevent a loss occurring and, if it happens, to **do what you can to prevent further damage**.

5 In the event of a claim, give **full and accurate information**, and **inform the insurance company immediately**.

6 **Make certain that you are adequately insured**.

7 Remember that **it is a crime to make a fraudulent claim**.

Chapter 3

Outdoor Security

It's all too easy to concentrate your attentions on fitting locks to windows and doors and to forget about external security altogether. You need to consider measures such as landscaping your property to prevent intruders from having places to hide, using security lighting to eliminate any 'black spots', and securing outbuildings.

A typical shed or garage will probably contain all the tools needed to break into your home – no matter how well-secured it might be. Neglecting the security of outbuildings could undo all the hard work you have put into securing your home.

Signs around your property that you are security-conscious will also help deter the would-be thief. If external security is up to scratch, the chances are that the home itself is also well protected. Even window stickers showing that you belong to a Neighbourhood Watch scheme, or ones declaring that your property is security-marked, may make an intruder think twice. 'Beware of the Dog' signs and dummy bell boxes can also play a role.

Design to fight crime

Landscape design is a very important security consideration and one which is often overlooked. With the introduction of the 'Secured by Design' concept for new housing projects, more thought has been put into estate design and many of these ideas can be adopted by individual home owners.

Perimeter protection

The type of property you live in will determine the level of perimeter protection required. A detached house, for instance, usually offers access to the rear, on both sides and at the back, requiring a higher level of protection.

A terraced house is more likely to provide limited access and a greater risk of being observed. If you live where your home can be clearly seen by neighbours or passers by, it's important to keep hedges or fences low so that any suspicious activity is likely to be observed.

Landscape design can also be used to protect more remote properties by restricting access, although obviously the home is more vulnerable if a burglar is not likely to be spotted attempting a break-in.

Homes which back on to open land, car parks, schools, or where there is easy access to the rear of the property, are particularly vulnerable. In such instances, protection may be provided by dense shrubbery, hedges, walls or fences.

A solid brick or stone wall, built to the maximum height permitted by the Local Authority, will provide a good level of protection, provided it does not feature decorative effects such as alcoves or projecting bricks which a burglar could use to scale the wall. Don't top the wall with broken glass or spikes. If there were an injury, you may be liable.

Iron railings also provide a reasonable barrier without limiting surveillance. Do, however, make sure that the

Keep fences low if your property can clearly be seen by neighbours or passers-by. (Fence by Jacksons Fine Fencing)

For security and convenience this gate has been fitted with an Autogate from Jacksons Fine Fencing, allowing automatic operation from the comfort of your car.

bars are close enough together – it could be a ten-year-old child trying to get in. Railings or a rose trellis can also be used to increase the height of a brick or stone wall. Wooden or wire fences provide little protection. They can easily be cut or kicked down.

Planting protection

Plants and shrubs can also be used to deter intruders. Roses or thorny shrubs can be planted in front of vulnerable windows, and shrubs with thorns or spikes can provide excellent perimeter protection. Keep them low to the ground, to provide clear views from neighbouring houses and pathways.

Paths to and from the house can also be used to improve security. A gravel drive or pathway makes a silent approach to your home difficult, increasing the burglar's risk of being spotted.

Side and rear access gates should always be firmly secured. Traditional garden gates are not very secure, with fixings and bolts that are often weak and easily overcome. Gates should be at least the same height as the surrounding wall or fence, and should provide minimum clearance at the bottom to prevent someone crawling under.

Ideally, the gate should be made of strong wood or metal, capable of standing up to a brute force attack, with no bars or rungs which a burglar could climb. Wrought iron gates often provide a ready-made climbing frame! Wooden gates should be secured with a five-lever mortise lock or a rim deadlock. Alternatively you could use a close shackle padlock in conjunction with a hasp and staple (also known as a padbar).

For large remote properties, security and convenience can be combined if you can afford the luxury of gates that open automatically. When these are linked to a closed circuit television camera (CCTV) and/or audio-visual entry panel, they enable you to view the caller and grant or refuse entry from the comfort of your own home. They also prevent a burglar getting a vehicle into your grounds, loading up and driving away.

Any CCTV system should be linked to a video recorder so that, if a break-in is attempted, the intruder will be captured on film. Cameras can also be strategically placed and linked together to provide surveillance for vulnerable areas around the home. Dummy CCTV cameras are also available to make a thief think that a system has been installed, or to make an existing system look more comprehensive than it really is.

Drainpipes

Drainpipes can provide a means of access to upstairs windows. Old metal drainpipes may be strong enough to climb and, provided the house is not listed, should be replaced with plastic versions. An alternative is to coat the drainpipe with anti-climb paint which should be applied from about 2m (6') upwards. This nasty, sticky substance will not dry, makes the pipe impossible to climb and leaves the intruder covered conspicuously in paint which is very difficult to remove.

Security lights

At night, a house that looks occupied, with lights on, immediately feels more secure than a house in darkness. Well positioned lighting is not only welcoming for you but will encourage the opportunist burglar to move on to where he can work in the shadows.

The simplest way to make the house look occupied is to leave a light on with the curtains drawn when you go out. And it really doesn't cost that much to keep a 60 watt bulb burning for a few hours. Even better, a modern compact fluorescent lamp bought for around £5 will cost about £4 per year to run if you switch it on every night. So don't just put in any old bulb, think about using the longer life lamps which will cost you less in the long run and you won't have to change them so often.

Good street lighting has been shown to reduce the fear of crime on large residential estates, making people feel safer and less worried about coming home to an empty house at night.

If you are unhappy about the lighting in your street, or perhaps a particular area close by, such as an underpass

Good street lighting can make a neighbourhood feel more secure and safer to live in.

or an alleyway, bring the matter up with your local Neighbourhood Watch scheme or the local authority. They may well be able to improve the situation, particularly if it is encouraging vandals, car thieves, burglary or similar criminal or antisocial activities.

You can do a great deal to improve your own lighting indoors and out but it is important to identify where it can be most effective. Apart from a light in the porch, it is important to illuminate dark corners at the side and back of the house. Be careful when you position the lights, as it is easy to create more shadows.

At the front door, the light should be mounted on the wall so that the caller is well lit. If it is mounted too high, you will find it not only awkward to change the lamp but it may also create a shadow. Ideally, the person answering the door should be in shadow, while the caller is bathed in light. If you have a door viewer fitted, it is pointless if you cannot see the caller through it at night.

If you have an existing outdoor light with mains wiring in place, then the job of fitting another light is very simple. If not, you may prefer to use a qualified electrician to do the initial work of providing a power supply.

If you feel confident to tackle it yourself (and aware that electricity is dangerous and can cause serious injury or death), then it is certainly possible to do all the work. Normally you can take power from the downstairs lighting circuit or, depending on where you want the light to be fixed, from the upstairs lighting circuit from the junction box or last loop-in ceiling rose. Before you start, turn off the electricity and isolate the circuit by removing the fuse from the consumer unit.

Using existing lights

You can convert existing lights into automatic security lights that switch on when someone approaches by fitting an internal controller. This lets you set how long the light remains on (from a few seconds to all the time) and adjust its sensitivity. It is operated by a passive infra-red sensor fitted outside to detect movement and both are wired to the existing light unit.

A number of sensors, sited at various points outside, can be linked to one control unit and these can also switch on a number of lights. Check the switching capacity, however, as they can vary from as low as 60W to 100W (for one light only) to 2,000W, and stay well within the manufacturer's recommendations.

The sensors should also be fitted with a photocell to prevent the light switching on in daylight. When incorporated in self-contained light units (ranging from lanterns to bulkhead lamps), this device offers an alternative to passive infra-red automatic lighting, switching them on automatically as light falls and off at dawn. So the lights are on all night rather than triggered when someone approaches.

Built-in sensors

As well as adding sensors to control existing lighting, you may prefer to fit a light which has a sensor built in. These range from floodlights (usually with 500W halogen lamps), ideal for lighting up the garden or a drive, to decorative coach lamps in different finishes – most popular are brass, white and black models.

Smiths SL032 Night Protector, a halogen floodlight operated using a passive infra-red detector.

A PIR can control existing lighting.

The Guardall Excalibur control unit for converting existing lights into automatic operation. A passive infra-red sensor fitted outside triggers the system.

A photocell-operated bulkhead light fitting from Superswitch.

If you need something with more resistance to attack, particularly for a vulnerable side of the house, choose a bulkhead light with vandal-resistant housing of poly-carbonate and concealed screws. Some floodlights can be supplied with protective grilles.

The passive infra-red units can usually be adjusted to alter the coverage provided. This is carried out by tilting the sensor head itself or by stick-on tapes provided by the manufacturer which enable you to mask the detection beam. For example, you may not wish people walking up the pathway next to your drive to switch on your light, so you can adapt the angle to allow for this.

To check that the light is operating correctly, most units will enable you to carry out a walk test before the unit is finally programmed. This will allow you to adjust the sensitivity angle and length of time on in daylight.

Sensors vary in their pattern of detection – most will have a range of at least 10m to 12m (30' to 36') and pick up movement across an angle of up to 180°; others may have a narrower angle and a shorter range. The manufacturers should provide this information on the packaging or literature.

You should also look for an IP rating indicating the unit's degree of resistance to moisture and dirt. The rates vary from IP33 at the lowest end to IP55 for the better models.

At the end of this chapter, we show you how to replace an existing lantern with an automatic passive infra-red operated model and a floodlight with a separate sensor.

Turn indoor lights into security lights by simply replacing the light switch:
(Top) The Audioswitch detects the sound of someone entering the room and switches the lights on.
(Centre) A miniature passive infra-red detects movement to trigger the light.
(Below) This unit simply repeats the light switching pattern of the previous 24 hours.

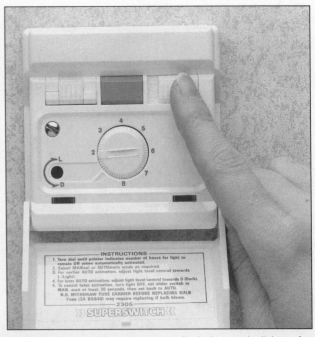

This light switch incorporates a photocell which turns the light on for up to eight hours after dusk.

Controlling indoor lamps

There is a wide range of devices which can control internal lighting. Plug-in timers allow you to control an electrical appliance, like a lamp or radio, to make the house look and sound occupied. They are plugged into the normal socket and the appliance then plugs into the timer. Some repeat the same switching patterns over 24 hours or can vary it from day to day on a seven-day cycle. Or there are timers designed to switch appliances on and off at pre-set times. Other units will switch on and off at random intervals.

Then there are replacement light switches. These replace the existing light switch and allow the lights to be activated by a variety of methods. For example, some can be programmed, just as the plug-in timers, while others remember when you switched on and off the day before and repeat the pattern, or they will switch the light on if a sound is heard or the device, using a passive infra-red detector, detects movement. They should include a photo-cell to ensure they don't come on during the day and allow you to switch back to manual control if necessary.

Until recently these switches have been limited to working with normal bulbs but a fluorescent light adaptor now on the market is for use with strip lighting (such as that often used in kitchens).

Other units – reacting to sound or with an in-built programme – simply plug into the bayonet of the lamp itself. The bulb then plugs into the device and is controlled by it.

Sunshine, size and simple installation!

Developments are reducing the size of sensors and making the units increasingly energy efficient. If you prefer to save your electricity, how about a light unit which uses the sun to power a rechargeable battery and is fitted with a long-life fluorescent bulb? It's a passive infra-red operated unit and can provide up to 14 days' power with no sun.

Many other lights can now use energy-saving bulbs, so it's worth shopping around. One of the smallest units on the market is a passive infra-red operated light about the size of a compact camera, which can be fitted neatly beneath guttering.

Wiring, too, is becoming less complex, with two-wire systems and low-voltage options making the job much easier.

We fitted a fully automatic quartz halogen security floodlight which has a passive infra-red attached. It has an adjustable detection range of up to 15m (45') with a coverage area of 180°. It can also switch up to 2,000W of additional lighting, so you could add more floodlights or lamps to the same system.

▶ **SEE PAGE 94 FOR STEP-BY-STEP INSTRUCTIONS ON FITTING AN AUTOMATIC LANTERN**

A plug-in timer shows the times you have programmed in for the lighting (or other appliance) to be switched on and off.

Another way of controlling a lamp. These units plug into the lamp between the bulb and the socket.

Sheds & Garages

The garage or shed probably contains not only the tools a burglar might need to break into your home but valuable garden equipment, sports gear and tools.

On all types of garages, you need to ensure that both the vehicle and personal access doors are secure. If you have an integral garage, it should be secured as part of the home. The door leading from the garage to the house should be treated as a final exit door and should be secured as a back door with a five-lever mortise lock and possibly hinge bolts and mortise bolts.

Detached garages should be secured with a five-lever mortise lock or deadlock on the personal access door. Metal 'up-and-over' doors are often supplied with low-grade locking devices which are easily overcome. These can be supplemented with a multi-purpose door bolt for metal or wooden doors which incorporates a steel locking bar designed to engage in a fixed frame and secured by a key.

Some up-and-over doors are now supplied with multi-point locking systems. Alternatively, one of the most successful ways of securing an up-and-over garage door is with a padbar and stout padlock fitted to each side of the metal door (use rivets to prevent tampering) and the bolt locking into the surrounding framework. For greater convenience, ask the locksmith for two close shackle padlocks that are keyed alike, so they can be operated

▶ SEE PAGE 96 FOR STEP-BY-STEP INSTRUCTIONS ON FITTING AN HALOGEN FLOODLIGHT

with the same key.

Garage doors can also be secured with a remote-controlled automatic opener if your budget will stretch to it. Double leaf doors may be secured with a cylinder rim lock but make sure that the door is in good condition – not weak or rotten. The second leaf should be fitted with bolts top and bottom, and hinge bolts should also be fitted to each side.

Garages and workshops may also be alarmed to provide greater protection. If part of the house, they may be linked in to the home alarm system, or incorporated into a wire-free system.

Alternatively, a battery-operated stand alone intruder alarm may be used, possibly with the additional protection of contact switches to protect doors and windows; and an additional siren can be fitted to the exterior of the garage or wired up inside the home to alert occupants to a break-in.

Sheds

Unfortunately, few sheds are designed for security. However, a burglar can often be deterred by a stout close-shackle padlock and padbar fitted to the door. Suitable window locks should also be fitted to shed and garage windows – again, make sure that the frames are in good condition.

Tools should be locked away in the shed or garage at all times, even if you are only popping out for a few minutes, so that they cannot be used for a break-in or

If you have an integral garage it should be secured as part of the home, with a 5-lever mortise lock and, ideally, mortise bolts and hinge bolts.

Small enough to fit under a gutter, this is the Trimalert, a 150W floodlight linked to a passive infra-red detector, from Homeguard UK.

vandalism. Items should also be security marked. Ladders in particular should be kept safely out of reach. If they cannot be locked in a garage, they can be fixed very securely to an outside wall with a roll bolt, length of chain and padlock.

Greenhouses

Even the garden greenhouse is not immune. Expensive plants can always be sold on – and no questions asked. A padlock on the door will help but, if your plants are really valuable, you could use a portable battery-operated alarm. This will sense an intruder and sound a loud, built-in alarm.

Padlocks

Padlocks vary tremendously in quality and, as usual, you get what you pay for. You will need not only a padlock but also a padbar which consists of a lock staple fitted to the door frame and a hinged hasp fitted to the door. For maximum security, choose a padlock with a concealed shackle or, next best, a close shackle and high shoulders.

A concealed or close shackle provides much greater resistance against attempts to cut or saw through the shackle. A shackle, which is easily accessible (i.e., an open shackle padlock) and which is not manufactured from hardened steel, provides an inferior level of protection as it is easily tampered with. To prevent tampering, the padlock and padbar should not have any exposed screws or bolt-heads (unless they are clutch head or security screws).

Fit good quality hasps and padlocks, ideally with a concealed or close shackle like the Diskus from CK Abus.

To ensure that the padlock is up to standard, look for the British Standard kitemark, which guarantees that it has been manufactured to meet the requirements of the British Standards Institute, or one which is 'insurance-approved'. Expect to pay around £20 upwards – very cheap padlocks offer little in the way of security.

▶ **SEE PAGE 98 FOR STEP-BY-STEP INSTRUCTIONS ON FITTING A GARAGE DOOR LOCK**

▶ **SEE PAGE 98 FOR STEP-BY-STEP INSTRUCTIONS ON FITTING A LADDER LOCK**

Garage doors can be opened and closed from the inside of your car with an automatic door opener.

For sheds and garages the Beta-Thief alarm incorporates two sirens – one to be used inside the protected property and the other fitted externally to be heard from nearby houses.

Don't leave ladders propped against a wall. Make sure they are properly secured.

Fitting an automatic lantern

Outside lights which switch on when someone approaches serve a dual purpose – they welcome the genuine visitor and deter those with dubious intent. They also let you to see your night-time caller without having to fumble for switches before opening the door.

Lights with built-in sensors range from floodlights, ideal for lighting up the garden or a drive, to the decorative coach lamp we install here. The most popular finishes are black, white and brass.

A passive infra-red unit can usually be adjusted to alter the coverage provided, while the unit's resistance to moisture and dirt is indicated by its IP number. Rates vary from IP33 at the lowest end to IP55 for the better models.

TOOLS AND MATERIALS

☐ Power drill + bits
☐ Hammer
☐ Screwdrivers
☐ Wire cutters
☐ Cable clips
☐ Electrical screwdriver

We fitted Smiths Industries SLO43 Brass Sensor Lantern, an automatic security/ courtesy light which incorporates a minia-ture passive infra-red detector. It has an 8m (24') detection range with a 180° coverage and will switch the lantern on for 2½ minutes. You can override this so that it is on permanently.

1 Unscrew the existing lantern and plinth, leaving the mains cable in position. Check the position of the new lamp, especially if you have overhanging porches or gutters. Here, we had to drop the cable down to the brickwork below the wooden fascia to accommodate the new lantern.

2 Using the lantern's plinth (or the template provided in the kit), mark the new position and the screw fixing holes. Drill the holes using a drill bit suitable for the material being drilled.

5 If working with brick, knock plugs into the drill holes with a hammer.

6 Press the rubber sealing grommet into the cable entry hole on the plinth base, using your fingers or a small screw driver to slip it into position.

7 Cut the mains cable to length, leaving enough to make the connections, run it into the plinth through the grommet. Screw the plinth into position with two No.8 40mm (1½") brass screws. Tack the cable with cable clips neatly into position.

8 Connect Live, Neutral and Earth from mains supply to lantern terminals (see manufacturer's diagram). The mains cable should be double insulated 3 core PVC sheathed cable 0.75 – 1mm.

9 Then connect the lantern by pushing the Live and Neutral leads on to the spade connections on the plinth base and secure the Earth lead to the Earth terminal – the lamp unit will be upside down at this stage.

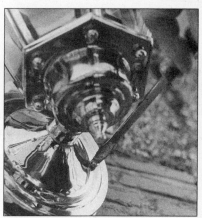

10 Swing the lamp upright and secure to the plinth with the two brass screws provided.

11 Fit a bulb (max. 100W) and remove the two brass cover screws from the top of the lantern base. Place the top cap in position and re-secure using the brass screws.

12 The walk test and operation are controlled from the mains switch indoors. After an initial walk test period, the lantern should set itself automatically. A sequence of on and off switching can be carried out to allow walk-testing or manual override.

13 Masking strips allow you to adjust the detection range and angle, but these are limited. Do a careful walk test, particularly if the door is at the side of the house! It responds better to people walking directly towards the sensor and should be mounted at a height of no more than 1.6 to 2m (5 to 6').

Fitting an automatic halogen floodlight

We fitted Smiths Night Protector (SL22), a fully automatic quartz halogen security floodlight which has a passive infra-red attached. It has an adjustable range of up to 15m (45'), covering an area of 180°. It can switch up to 2,000W of additional lighting, so you could add more floodlights or lamps to the system. When setting up floodlights, make sure you don't create a lighting nuisance for your neighbours, by shining brightly into their living or bedroom windows, for example.

TOOLS AND MATERIALS

- ☐ Power drill + bits
- ☐ Hammer
- ☐ Screwdrivers
- ☐ Wire cutters
- ☐ Cable clips
- ☐ Electrical screwdriver

1 This was the old lamp at the rear of the house. Its only good point was that the mains wiring was already available!

2 The components of the Night Protector.

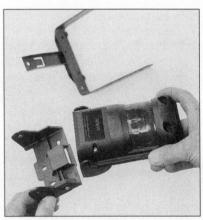

3 The passive infra-red unit slots into the brackets provided and sits below the floodlight.

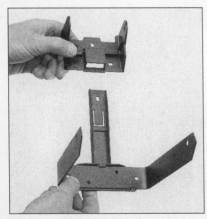

4 The brackets for the passive infra red and floodlight also slot together.

5 Having clicked the brackets for the sensor unit and lamp together, ensuring the lamp fixing holes are at the top of the bracket, mark the wall for drilling. Make sure it is square or it could look a real eyesore.

6 Drill the holes using a suitable drill, and plug if going into mortar.

7 Remove the top cover on the halogen lamp. The cable which links the sensor to the halogen lamp is supplied. Strip the wires first.

8 Feed the Neutral, Live and Earth from the sensor unit through the grommet into the lamp unit. Connect the earth link to the tab screw by squeezing with pliers. For easier installation, remove the terminal block before connecting the Live and Neutral wires.

9 Screw terminal block back into position and replace cover.

10 Connect the cable from the lamp to the appropriate terminals as marked in the sensor housing.

11 Screw the lamp and sensor bracket into position on the wall.

12 Using the hexagon nuts provided, secure the lamp to the bracket; the sensor will be hanging below it.

13 Clip the sensor into its bracket below the lamp.

14 Bring the mains cable to the sensor unit and wire as indicated (the two earth wires will be in the same terminal).

15 Screw the cable clamps into position to hold the wiring in place. The grommets provide protection against weather and a seal prevents dirt getting in.

16 Fix the sensor housing with the two screws provided.

17 You can adjust light level sensitivity and time the lamp stays on by turning the controls with a screw driver.

18 The installed floodlight is adequate to illuminate a small garden; additional lights can be run from the same system.

Fitting a garage door lock

TOOLS AND MATERIALS

- ☐ Power drill + bits
- ☐ Rivet gun + rivets
- ☐ Pencil

1 Mark and drill holes on the garage door for the padbar.

2 Secure bar in position with bolts that cannot be undone from the outside.

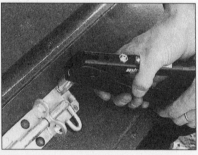

3 With the bolts holding the padbar firmly in position, use a the rivet gun to shoot rivets through remaining screw holes.

4 Using a pencil or sharp instrument, mark the position of the bolt hole on the garage wall and drill.

5 Slide bolt into the wall and secure with a stout padlock. Repeat for the other side of the door.

Fitting a ladder lock

TOOLS AND MATERIALS

- ☐ Power drill + masonry bits
- ☐ Adjustable spanner

1 Select a suitable site for the roll bolt, indoors or out, and drill hole.

2 Insert the bolt to check fit – the drill hole must be just the right size to accept the bolt.

OUTSIDE
WATCH POINTS

1 **Make sure your house can be clearly seen** by neighbours and passers-by.

2 Houses which back on to open land should be **secured with high walls or dense shrubbery**.

3 Use prickly shrubs outside windows to **deter intruders**.

4 Make sure gates are the same height as the surrounding wall and provide **minimum clearance** at the bottom.

5 Secure garage doors, gates, sheds and greenhouses with **adequate locking devices**.

6 Ideally, use higher security **close shackle padlocks.**

7 **Replace metal drainpipes** with plastic ones if they provide easy access to upstairs windows.

8 On an integral garage treat the personal access door as a **final exit door** and **secure with a five-lever mortise lock**.

3 Once the fit is correct, insert the roll bolt and secure in place by tightening the nut.

4 Loop chain through the ring on the bolt, around the ladder several times and secure in place with the padlock.

Chapter 4

Personal Security

The chances of becoming a victim of violent crime are remote but, for some people, the fear of it can be very real; it can even make them prisoners in their own homes. Women and the elderly tend to feel vulnerable, while children, by their very innocence, can be seen as easy prey. In reality, though, it is young men who are mainly the victims of violent crime.

Violent crime is largely about power and the need to dominate a victim. Research has actually shown that people are more likely to become a victim if they walk along looking nervous and vulnerable. Someone who appears confident and self-assured is less likely to be attacked.

Obviously it doesn't pay to take unnecessary risks. Simple forward planning and common-sense precautions can often avoid a potentially dangerous situation and make you feel safer when out and about. What is important is to think ahead; think about what you would do in the event of an attack; be alert and go about your everyday life with confidence.

you have only just met – no matter how genuine he may seem, and never, never hitch-hike; far better to travel home with someone you know well. If your house is empty, ask your friends or the taxi driver to wait until you are safely inside. If you regularly have to work late, ask your company whether they can arrange transport for you or arrange a lift rota with colleagues.

If you must travel home alone at night, always avoid short-cuts through dimly-lit, deserted areas and alleyways. Walk in the centre of the pavement, keeping away from bushes and dark buildings, and walk facing the oncoming traffic. This makes it difficult for a kerb-crawler to follow you.

If you regularly go out walking or running, vary your route and time, so that people do not get to know your routine. Choose well-lit, well-populated routes and avoid using a personal stereo; not only will it prevent you hearing someone approaching, it could also leave you vulnerable to a snatch-thief.

Handbags should be kept closed and carried close to your body, and should never be left unattended in public places. Purses should be pushed towards the bottom of

Out alone

Much of this advice is aimed at women but men should be aware of these simple precautions, too. If you are going to be out late on your own, always take steps to ensure that you can get home safely. Arrange a lift home with friends or book a taxi in advance. Try to use a firm you know well or a licensed cab company.

If you must use an unlicensed minicab, when you phone, ask for the driver's name and call sign and the type of car he will be driving. When he turns up, check that he knows your name. Always sit in the back and, if you do feel uneasy, trust your instincts and ask him to drop you off at the nearest busy place.

Never accept lifts from someone

If you are going to be out late on your own, always take steps to ensure that you can get home safely.

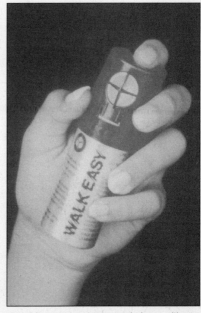

Consider carrying a personal alarm – like the 'Walk Easy'.

the bag to guard against theft. Similarly, men should never carry their wallets in rear trouser pockets. Expensive-looking jewellery should be covered up until you reach your destination.

Many women feel safer by carrying a personal alarm. In the event of an attack, the alarm can be operated easily to sound a piercing screech, which may frighten off your attacker, and will also alert anyone in the vicinity that you are being attacked.

These small devices are either gas or battery-operated and cost from around £5. Gas-operated alarms are louder but, if you buy one, make sure that when the top is depressed to sound the alarm, it will lock in position. That way, even if it is dropped, the alarm will continue to sound. Whichever type you buy, test it regularly to make sure that it is operating correctly and, when you are out and about, make sure it is ready to hand – not buried at the bottom of your handbag!

Public transport

Try to avoid being alone on public transport. Avoid isolated bus stops and, if possible, unmanned, isolated railway stations. On the bus, sit on the lower deck near the driver, and on trains and tubes, avoid empty compartments. If you can, sit in a part of the train near where you get off and try to sit near other women whenever possible. Trust your instincts at all times. If you are sitting in a compartment with plenty of spare seats, and a man gets on and sits down next to you, making you feel uneasy, then move. Do not worry about offending him!

Men can play a part to help women feel safer. Think about how a woman may feel if, for instance you are walking quite close behind her in a secluded area. Simply by crossing the road and walking on the other side you can reassure her that she is safe. Similarly, do not sit too near a woman on her own in a railway carriage, unless there are plenty of people. Finally, help women friends and family members by offering them lifts or walking them home.

In the car

Although there has been a considerable increase in the number of women drivers in recent years, it is still an unfortunate fact that women are more likely than men to be the subject of unwelcome attention when driving alone. There's no reason to think that driving alone spells trouble but it's a good idea to take certain precautions which will help to avoid finding yourself in an unpleasant situation.

Make sure your car is in good running order at all times and is regularly serviced. This will minimise the possibility of a breakdown. Make sure that you know how to change a wheel and make sure that the car jack is in good condition in case you have a puncture.

If the car is playing up and you think it may break down, find an alternative means of transport or take someone with you. Lessons in basic car maintenance will at least give you the confidence to tackle smaller jobs, such as a puncture or broken fan belt.

When driving in towns, keep the doors locked and your handbag out of sight or on the floor. Do not leave it on the passenger seat where it could easily be snatched. Avoid attracting unnecessary attention, avoid 'jokey' stickers in car windows, which may encourage unwelcome attention, and avoid eye contact with 'undesirables'. Beware of other drivers trying to alert you to

Trust your instincts when using public transport. If you feel threatened by someone's behaviour, report it to a guard, or other member of staff.

At night check the inside of your car with a torch before you get in.

faults with your car. Drive on slowly until you reach a place where it is safe to stop and then check your car.

If you think you're being followed, pull over and slow down, but don't stop. Don't drive to your home but find a busy and well lit place. If the person following persists, blow your horn and flash your lights to attract attention.

If you're stopped by traffic or another vehicle, lock the doors and close the windows. Don't ram the other vehicle - damage to your car might prevent your escape.

If you're travelling a long way or on an unfamiliar route, make a few notes before you set off, reminding yourself of the road numbers, where to turn, which junctions to use on motorways, etc. Try to stick to busy roads where possible. Always carry an up-to-date road atlas and local maps of your destination area so you won't have to stop to ask directions.

Make sure that you have enough petrol for the journey. If you need to fill up during the journey, make sure that you do so in plenty of time, before the fuel level gets too low and before petrol stations close if you're travelling at night.

Always carry some change or a phone card so you can make a phone call if necessary. If you think that your family or friends may be worried, it's a good idea to phone someone at your destination before setting off to tell them that you're leaving and what time you expect to arrive. Similarly, when you arrive, you may want to phone someone at your starting point to confirm that you've arrived safely.

Many drivers (male and female) are now using personal or on-board mobile phones. These systems are not cheap but prices are coming down and the expense may well be worth the reassurance it gives you and your family in the long term.

It goes without saying that you should never pick up hitch-hikers. If somebody does flag you down, make sure that it is a genuine emergency before opening your door or winding down the window. If you are in any doubt, drive on to the nearest telephone or police station and report the incident.

When parking, look for a well-lit, preferably busy area. If you park in a car park, try to park close to an exit or close to the attendant's station. Always reverse into the parking space so that you can drive away quickly if necessary after returning to your car.

Always lock your car and look for landmarks so that you can find your car quickly when you return.

When you leave your car, try not to leave any clues that the car is being driven by a woman. Driving shoes, sunglasses, a scarf or hat - these can all betray the driver's gender. Make sure that anything of a feminine nature is removed or hidden from sight before leaving your car.

When you return, walk with a group of people, if possible. Have the keys ready so that you don't have to spend unnecessary time outside your car searching for them, which may attract attention.

Before getting into your car, briefly check for forced entry and look into the car for any suspicious signs. Don't get into the car if you notice anything suspicious.

The fact is you are far more likely to be injured in an accident than a personal attack. Even so, if you do have a breakdown, you will still want to summon help as quickly as possible. Always walk to phone for assistance, don't accept a lift. When you phone for assistance, mention that you're an unaccompanied woman.

If someone stops while you're phoning, give the operator details of the other vehicle's registration number and a brief description of the car and driver. If the driver

There are alarms available for the elderly which are designed to summon help in an emergency – like the Homelink from Scantronic.

If you are assaulted or raped, call the police straightaway. They are trained to deal with such situations.

approaches you, tell them that you have passed on his/her details to the police. If the driver's intentions are honourable, your reaction will be understood.

It really does pay to join a motoring organisation such as the AA or RAC, as they will give priority to lone women drivers. Even if you are not a member, they will help you provided you are willing to join there and then.

If you break down on the motorway, pull on to the hard shoulder and follow the marker arrows to the nearest phone – try to get your car as near to one as possible. After you have called, wait on the embankment near your car, leaving the nearside door unlocked and slightly open, so that you can get inside quickly to lock yourself in if necessary. If you decide to stay inside the car, sit in the passenger seat and lock the door - this keeps you as far away as possible from passing traffic and also gives the impression that you're accompanied.

'HELP – CALL POLICE' signs, available from some motoring shops, have been successful in summoning assistance. Placed in your rear window, the idea is that passing motorists will use their car phones to contact the police on your behalf or stop at the nearest telephone to summon assistance. If someone offers assistance, get into your car, lock the door, open the window a fraction and tell them the police have been informed and are arranging recovery. However, if you have not yet contacted the police, consider asking the person to do so on your behalf. If you are at all uncertain about the person's intentions, tell them that the police are aware and ask them to call the police again for you.

When help arrives, ask for some form of identification (even from a policeman) before giving any of your own details.

Should you be involved in an accident, it is important to keep calm. If you should be bullied or shouted at by another driver, lock yourself in your car (if it's safe to do so) and wind the windows up. Communicate through a small gap at the top of the window. If things get out of hand, refuse to talk to anyone except the police.

If you would like further practical help, several organisations (some local police authorities, AA, etc.) run courses especially for women drivers, in which subjects such as basic car maintenance and self defence are covered.

Home alone

Even in your own home, don't take chances. Security locks should be fitted to all doors and windows – and used! External doors should be kept locked even when you are indoors. Door locks should be changed when you

HOME ALONE
WATCHPOINTS

1	Fit and use **security locks on doors and windows** – even when you are home.
2	**Draw the curtains after dark**.
3	Do not advertise the fact that you live alone.
4	**Never give out your number on the telephone**.
5	If you suspect there is a prowler or intruder at the house, **phone the police immediately**.
6	Do not admit strangers without **checking their identity** carefully.

PERSONAL
WATCHPOINTS

1 At night, arrange for transport to **get you home safely**.

2 **Avoid** walking through **dimly-lit, deserted areas and alleys**.

3 Try to walk **facing oncoming traffic** and in the **middle of the pavement**.

4 **Never hitch-hike, or pick up hitch-hikers**.

5 **Conceal expensive-looking jewellery**.

6 Try to **avoid being alone on public transport**, and at bus stops and train stations.

7 Make sure your car is in **good working order**.

8 **Join** a motoring organisation such as the **AA or RAC**.

9 **Keep car doors locked** in town, and your handbag out of sight.

10 **Park in well-lit, populated places** – preferably near the ground floor exit in multi-storey car parks.

11 Consider buying a **personal alarm**.

move to a new home in case previous tenants still have keys that fit. Always draw your curtains after dark and, if you suspect there is a prowler outside, dial 999 immediately. Should you arrive home and suspect that your house has been broken into, do not enter. Run to a neighbour's house and call the police.

Do not advertise the fact that you live alone. Display only your surname and initials in telephone directories or by your doorbell so that a stranger will not know whether there is a male or female occupant.

If you are selling your home, try to avoid situations where you have to show viewers around on your own. Either ask the estate agent to accompany the viewer or arrange for someone to be at home with you.

Wrong number

When you answer the phone, never give out your number. If you use an answerphone machine, never imply in your message that you are out of the house. Say something along the lines of 'We're sorry we can't take your call at the moment…' Ask a male friend or relative to record the message for you.

If a stranger telephones, never admit that you are on your own. If calls are obscene or abusive, hang up without saying a word – the caller is after a response. If the calls continue, tell the police and the operator. Keep a record of the date, time and content of each call to help the authorities trace the caller. If you dial '1471' immediately after receiving the call, BT's 'Call Return' service may be able to identify the caller's number for you. But do not, in any circumstances, call this number back. Give the information to the police and let them handle the matter.

The elderly

Most of these precautions apply to the elderly as well but the elderly are also particularly vulnerable to doorstep tricksters. Elderly relatives should be discouraged from keeping large sums of money at home – this should always be deposited in a bank, building society or post office account.

Alarms for the elderly and infirm, which offer protection against burglary and summon help in an emergency, are discussed in detail in the chapter on alarms.

If the worst happens

It's always wise to be prepared for the worst. Preparing yourself mentally could help you to think rationally should the situation occur, rather than just freezing with fear.

Some women find that a self-defence class, targeted specifically for women, makes them feel more confident. But, in terms of actually fighting off an attacker, shock and fear may make you forget what you have been taught, so the fact that you have attended classes should not lead you to take unnecessary risks.

If you think someone is following you, cross the street. If he continues, run to the busiest place you can find. A description of the man will help the police track him down but your priority should be to get away safely. Incidents such as these should be reported as soon as possible from a safe place. Do not use a phone box in the street as you could be trapped inside.

Should you be confronted by a flasher, try not to appear shocked. Simply walk away and report the incident to the police, with the most detailed description that you can manage. If you are threatened or confronted by a stranger, shout or scream for help.

To protect yourself against an attack, you are allowed to use reasonable force. You may use everyday items to fight off an attacker, such as keys, hairspray, an umbrella – anything which you would normally carry with you.

The law does not permit you to carry a knife, mace spray or anything that can be described as an offensive weapon. If you are assaulted or raped, call the police straightaway. Do not wash until a doctor has seen you and do not drink or clean your teeth as this could destroy vital evidence.

Try to remember as much as possible about the attack – write it down if possible. The police are trained to deal with such situations and to provide you with care and understanding. They can also put you in touch with counsellors who can offer valuable assistance to you and your family. Rape Crisis Centres or Victim Support Schemes can help you cope with an attack and Social Services can help if you or your children need to get away from a violent person.

Keeping children safe

Children are naturally trusting and, unless warned, will quite happily talk to complete strangers. But it is not only strangers who are a danger; most child molesters know their victims – they may be relatives, family friends, neighbours or someone else who the victim is often in contact with. That's why it is vital that children know that it is OK to say NO to anyone – stranger or friend – and that parents can recognise the danger signals.

Children should be taught never to go off with anyone without asking Mummy or Daddy first. But strangers are cunning. Unless a child is taught otherwise, it is very easy for them to get in a car with someone who claims that 'Mummy sent me because she isn't feeling well'.

If you do ask someone else to collect your child from school, tell the class teacher who will be coming. It is also a good idea to give the collector a password that the child recognises so that they know the person is genuine. With very young children, even if you are only going to be ten minutes or so late, it is advisable to tell the school - young children can quickly become unnerved if life doesn't go to pattern and may react unpredictably.

Your child should also know that, if a stranger asks for help (to find a lost dog or for directions, for instance), the child should still say NO, run away and tell you or another known adult or police officer about the incident immediately. They do not need to give the adult an explanation – NO is sufficient.

Make sure the child understands that nobody has the right to touch their bodies. If the child asks unusual questions about somebody or shows fear when a particular person is coming round, do not ignore it – follow up on the questions. And if a child does tell you that someone has interfered with them, believe them – children rarely lie about such incidents.

Often a molester will tell the child to keep the incident a secret. Make sure your children know the difference between good and bad secrets. Bad secrets are if someone has hurt them or tried to take them away or touched them where they shouldn't. Bad secrets should not be kept secret.

CHILDREN
WATCHPOINTS

1 Teach children that it is OK to say **NO to anyone who tries to hurt them**.

2 Make sure they know **never to go off with anyone** without telling you first.

3 Children must be taught that **no-one has the right** to touch their bodies.

4 **Believe your child** if they tell you someone has interfered with them.

5 Teach your child that there are **some secrets that should never be kept**.

6 Ensure you know **where your child is**, **who they are with** and **the time they are expected home**.

7 Teach children **not** to answer the front door.

8 Teach them that it is OK to **run, scream, shout, lie or kick** to get away.

9 Make sure the child knows its **address and phone number**.

10 Don't send a child out with its **name** displayed on a badge or T-shirt. They may be confused if a stranger calls them by name.

11 Use someone you know well, or who has been well-recommended for **babysitting**.

12 **Never hesitate to call the police** if you are concerned about your child's whereabouts.

It's important that you know at all times where your child is, who they are with and the time that they are expected home. Children should be taught to give you this information as a matter of course. Neither should they be allowed in anyone's house – even a friend's – without notifying you first.

If they are not home by the allocated time, investigate immediately. The police would rather have a false alarm than a potential tragedy. Make sure that children know their own address and how to use a pay phone, and how to make reverse charge calls before they are allowed out without an adult. And when at home, they should be taught never to answer a call at the front door.

Finding a reliable, trustworthy baby-sitter can be difficult. Where possible, ask a friend or member of your family or ask friends if they can recommend someone they have used. Try to avoid using newspaper advertisements. Leave a number where you can be contacted and ring home and ask to speak to your child if you are worried. Finally, be aware of the danger signs. Watch your child's reaction when he or she knows a baby-sitter is coming. If they react badly, don't take any chances. Far better to be safe than sorry.

Milk bottles collecting on the doorstep, and post sticking out of the letter box is an obvious indication that you are away.

Holidays & Travel

Holiday preparations leave most people in a last-minute panic. Hunting around for passports, checking insurance details…. No wonder you start worrying whether you forgot to lock the back door or cancel the papers or the milk. And these are the just signs the thief looks for, especially during the holiday season.

Advance planning with a simple holiday checklist can ease the worries. The main objective is to deter a burglar from approaching your home in the first place. So it is important the house continues to look occupied while you are away.

Milk bottles collecting on the doorstep, post sticking out of the letter box and a house in darkness at night are all tell-tale signs that you are away. Cancelling the milk and papers sounds obvious but a surprising number of people do forget – particularly if they are only going away for a weekend.

Don't rely on a spoken agreement – make sure that the cancellation is written in the order book. To avoid a build-up of post you can, for a fee, arrange for the Post Office to hold it for you until you return. However, this does not prevent the delivery of leaflets and free sheets which are often not pushed fully through the letter box.

Good neighbours

Your best course of action is to enlist the help of neighbours. Leave them a key and they can collect your post for you, draw the curtains and switch the lights on, leave the dustbin out and possibly even mow the grass. You can also suggest they park on your driveway to make the home look occupied. And you can, of course, always return the favour when they go away.

If you live in a Neighbourhood Watch area, your neighbours should be well aware of the importance of making sure neighbouring residences look occupied and should be happy to help. It's a good idea to contact the local Neighbourhood Watch co-ordinator and leave them a key, as well as an address where you can be contacted.

He or she can then keep an eye on your property, report anything suspicious to the police, and ensure that you can be contacted if anything untoward occurs. The local police should also be informed of your absence.

Homesitters

If you cannot or do not want to enlist the help of your friends or neighbours, there are agencies around that offer a home-minding service. Basically, for a fee, these agencies will send people round to live in and look after

HOLIDAY CHECKLIST

Before you go away have you remembered to...

1 Cancel the milk? .... ☐

2 Cancel newspaper deliveries? .... ☐

3 Ensure that cancellations are written in the order book? ☐

4 Arrange for the Post Office and/or neighbours to
keep your post for you? .... ☐

5 Ask neighbours to keep an eye on your home? .... ☐

6 Contact the local Neighbourhood Watch co-ordinator? . ☐

7 Leave an address where you can be contacted? .... ☐

8 Inform local police of your absence? .... ☐

9 Lock all windows and doors? .... ☐

10 Lock the garage and shed? .... ☐

11 Lock away ladders? .... ☐

12 Set the Intruder alarm? .... ☐

13 Instruct a neighbour or keyholder on how the intruder
alarm operates? .... ☐

14 Activate security lighting devices – inside and out? ..... ☐

15 Move valuable objects out of sight? .... ☐

16 Lock small valuable objects and credit cards away safely? ☐

your house while you are away and, for an additional charge, look after pets as well.

Usually you are also expected to pay the homesitter and provide expenses. The local Crime Prevention Officer may have information on agencies operating in your area; or try Yellow Pages or the Thomson Local Directory. Do be careful, though, as you may have no means of knowing how reputable the people appointed to look after your home may be.

Don't tell too many people you're going away. Thieves can pick up casual conversations in pubs, restaurants and shops and use the information. Luggage must be labelled in case of loss but avoid attaching your home address to the outside of the case. Criminals are on the lookout for such information – it is an obvious indication that your home is likely to be unoccupied for one or two weeks and this information can be passed on to accomplices and used. Label your bags with your destination and put your home address inside the case or put the address of your office on the label so, in the event of loss, luggage can be returned to you safely.

If you have an answerphone, word the message carefully so it is not possible to ascertain that you are on holiday.

Safe and secure

Apart from these common-sense precautions, remember to use any home security devices that have been installed - strong locks on all external doors and accessible windows, locks and padlocks on the garage, shed and ladders, alarm systems activated, keyholders, neighbours and monitoring service notified.

Some Neighbourhood Watch schemes have portable alarms which may be loaned to neighbours when they go away. These alarms are designed to protect a room or entrance hall, sensing movement or heat change and, in response, activating a built-in siren.

Lighting-up time

Security lighting is invaluable when you are going away for any length of time. There are various devices available which will switch your lights on and off. More sophisticated ones work on a random principle and, installed in several rooms, can give the impression that an entire family is home. Exterior security lighting also ensures that intruders risk being spotted by neighbours or passers-by.

For holiday use, some time-switches can be programmed to turn the lights on and off at random intervals over a seven-day period – daylight operation is prevented by a sensor device. Time switches may also be used to control a variety of electrical appliances. By connecting one to a radio, for instance, you could use sound as a deterrent as well.

If you leave lights or electrical appliances on in an empty house, keep them well away from curtains or inflammable materials or a fire could result.

Safekeeping

Valuable items like antiques, hi-fi equipment, televisions and videos should be moved out of sight of prying eyes when you go away.

If you have a safe, small objects can be locked away securely. Alternatively you may wish to pay to deposit them at a bank for safekeeping. Any credit cards which you are not taking with you should also be locked away safely.

Leave keys with a friend or neighbour – never in a supposedly 'safe' place.

Remember to close and securely lock all windows and doors.

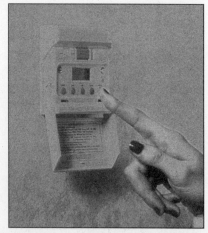

Use a programmable light switch to switch lights on and off while you are away. This model from Superswitch operates lights at preset times over a seven-day period.

HOLIDAY WATCHPOINTS

1	Take steps to make sure **your home looks occupied**.
2	**Cancel all deliveries** and ensure this is noted in the order book.
3	Enlist the help of **friends, family and neighbours**.
4	**Leave a key with a neighbour**, and an address where you can be contacted.
5	**Take care not to inform too many people of your forthcoming absence**.
6	Make sure **home security is up to scratch**, and that **devices are used**.

Holiday homes

Homes that are only used for holiday purposes are particularly difficult to keep secure. If it is on a site, there may be adequate security, but a property on its own, or surrounded by other holiday properties, could be an easy target.

In such cases, it is important to ensure is nothing left worth stealing. Strip the property internally and leave the curtains open, so an intruder can see inside, and leave all the drawers and cupboards empty and open.

Locks should be fitted to all doors and windows but, if the property is in a remote location where an intruder is likely to have more time to break in, a higher level of security can be provided with the installation of grilles or shutters.

External security measures will also help, along the lines of those in the section on outdoor security.

Try to ensure that all mail relating to the property is sent to your main address.

Travel security

The best of holidays can become a nightmare with the loss of cash or credit cards, clothing or valuables. So try to avoid taking items of real value with you. Any jewellery should be costume jewellery and credit cards should be kept to a minimum.

Before you set off, write out a list of what you are carrying in your luggage to assist you should you need to make an insurance claim. Keep a record of the numbers of all credit cards, your passport and driving licence, and carry a copy with you, separate from your luggage, leaving another safely at home with someone you trust. Also carry telephone numbers with you to report credit card losses immediately.

Packed to go

Always keep valuables, such as money, documents, jewellery, cameras and electrical goods, in your hand luggage so that it stays with you at all times. Be prepared for your luggage to get lost in transit by carrying a few essentials in your hand luggage, such as a change of clothing and some toiletries. Keep your hand luggage zipped up or fastened at all times, and your wallets in inside pockets to deter thieves who operate at airports, coach stations and ports.

Choose suitcases for their strength, security and convenience rather than appearance. Bear in mind that soft-sided cases can be torn in transit, especially with air travel, whilst those with a stiffer construction can split if dropped. Check that locking devices operate securely. Padlock zipped cases, and use luggage straps to provide additional security, and to keep your possessions in place should the case burst open. Use address labels as advised above.

Do not let your luggage out of your sight. Never ask a stranger to keep an eye on it for you and never agree to look after someone else's luggage for them. Suppose it went missing whilst in your care or was found to contain drugs or firearms!

At your destination

Most hotels offer a safe deposit facility where you can leave cash, valuables and important documents. Items such as these should never be left in an empty hotel room, even if it is locked, unless the room itself is fitted with a safe.

Many of the rules for personal safety at home apply in your hotel room. Keep the door locked at all times and, if there is a knock at the door, do not open it until you have identified the caller. If there is a door chain and door viewer fitted, use them. If the caller claims to be carrying out repairs on behalf of the hotel or making a delivery, phone the front desk and check before admitting him.

Keys should be left at the front desk whenever you go out – not carried with you. Close and secure all accessible windows when you go out. Portable personal door locks are now available in the UK to provide additional protection. These can be used only when the room is occupied to increase personal safety or to provide additional privacy for bathrooms.

If, when you get to your hotel room, you think a burglar is inside, do not enter. Go down to the front desk and report it. If you awake to find someone in your room, do not pretend to be asleep. Yell, scream and call the front desk.

On the day of departure, do not leave packed luggage unattended in your room. Ask the hotel to keep it safely for you. Finally, make sure you and your family are aware of fire procedure in the hotel and know which exits to use. NEVER use the lift in the event of a fire.

Campers and caravans should be locked up when you are inside at night, and should be properly secured when you leave them (see Chapter 5). Avoid leaving valuables in an unoccupied camper. If you are going on a camping holiday, don't take any items of value with you unless they are absolutely essential. Money and other valuables should be kept with you at all times. If you must take items of value, lock them away in the boot of your car and set the vehicle alarm.

Out and about

There are numerous common-sense precautions to bear in mind when travelling at home or abroad. Women travelling alone or with a few friends should follow the same safety procedures that they would at home (see Chapter 2). Carry bags close to your side, with the clasp towards you, and with your purse tucked right away out of reach. Never walk back to your hotel or apartment alone at night and never hitch-hike or accept lifts from strangers.

It's always a good idea to find out something about your holiday destination before you make your booking. Ask the travel agent whether the area is regarded as safe or contact the tour company. There are guide books available which are written specifically for women travelling alone or together.

To avoid attracting attention, British tourists in Florida have been advised to personalise their hire cars with stickers so they don't look too new. It's important not to leave valuables in the car. If you get lost while driving, make your way to a safe place such as a garage or police station to ask for directions, rather than asking a passer-by.

Do not study maps while driving. Luggage should be locked away out of sight and doors should be kept locked

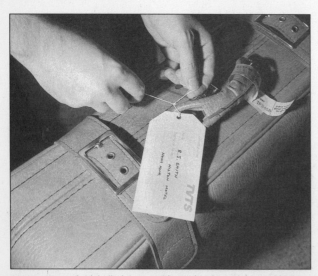

Luggage must be labelled, but avoid attaching your home address to the outside of your case.

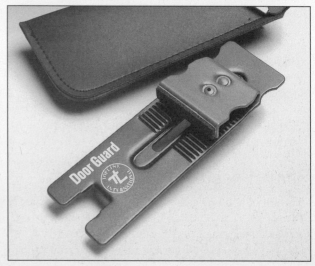

Portable personal door locks, like Doorguard can be used to increase personal safety.

when driving and parked. If someone tries to 'nudge' your car or make you stop, drive on to a busy, well-lit area and call the police.

You can reduce the risk of being attacked by trying to blend in. Dress down, don't wear valuable jewellery and keep cameras and video cameras hidden. Carry a map and make sure you know exactly where you are going so that you avoid dangerous neighbourhoods.

Money matters

Most thieves will be after money. Avoid carrying a lot of cash – just enough for emergencies and casual expenditure. Ideally, use travellers' cheques and credit cards. Always follow the instructions issued with travellers' cheques and keep a record of the serial numbers – but not with the cheques. Cross each serial number off as you use the cheques so, in the event of loss or theft, you know which ones are missing.

Money, cheques and credit cards must be carried safely, out of reach of casual pickpockets. A money belt provides good security, worn around your waist under your clothes, or around your wrist or ankle for use on the beach. Make sure you understand the currency well enough to avoid pulling out huge wads of notes or travellers' cheques.

If you can, avoid carrying all your money with you at one time. In a hotel, it should be deposited in the safe. Keep credit card receipts safely so that no-one can find out your number and, when you use your card, make sure that it is returned to you – not swapped for another. Try to carry travellers' cheques and credit cards separately so, if one is stolen, you will still have access to some funds.

Business travellers

Business travel often involves carrying round expensive office-type equipment, such as laptop computers and mobile phones, as well as valuable demonstration equipment. Laptops are often carried in custom-made cases which do little to disguise what they are.

Try to limit the amount you take with you to hand luggage only, so it can be carried with you at all times, and make sure that bags and cases are secured with strong locks. Expensive equipment should be disguised or concealed in a bag or locked in the boot of a car, preferably with a vehicle alarm in operation.

Make sure that vehicle insurance covers theft of personal and business property. Ask your hotel if they have a large safe where you could deposit demonstration equipment. Portable intruder alarms are also available, which may be used in a hotel room to detect an intrusion, or a door alarm which, fixed to the door, will sense it opening and sound the alarm.

Insurance

When travelling in the UK, you may find that your house contents insurance provides coverage for property lost or stolen outside the home. When travelling abroad, however, it's a good idea to take out separate holiday insurance to cover your belongings for loss or damage while travelling and during your holiday. The policy will also cover you for personal accident, medical expenses, travel delay, travel cancellation and personal liability. Carry the paper work with you while you are away.

When taking out holiday insurance, read the small print carefully – don't just accept the travel agent's word – make sure that the policy provides adequate cover and

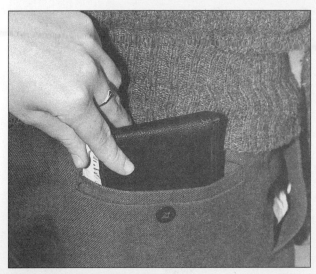

To deter pickpockets, do not keep wallets in a trouser back pocket.

Hold on to handbags. Do not tuck them away where you cannot see them.

that the maximum amount per any one item is sufficient.

It pays to shop around. You will need about £1,500 cover for personal belongings, enough cover for the money you are taking with you, £250,000 cover for medical expenses in Europe (or £1,000,000 in the USA and the rest of the world), cover for the full cost of your holiday and £1,000,000 personal liability cover in all countries except the USA, where you will need at least £2,000,000.

You will probably be expected to pay an 'excess' if you make a claim – usually the first £25. Bear in mind also that standard holiday insurance only provides indemnity cover, i.e., if you lose something the insurance company will only pay the second-hand replacement value. If your house contents provides new-for-old all-risks cover, you may be able to claim under this.

Health care

Britain has a restricted reciprocal health care arrangement with other countries. If you are visiting an EC country, complete an EIII form (available from the Department of Health and Social Security and many Post Offices). This form must accompany you when you travel and be presented if you require treatment.

However, it's worth taking out separate medical insurance, as it won't cover the cost of bringing someone back to the UK in the event of death or illness, and it only covers state hospitals. There are other restrictions in individual countries. If you claim medical expenses, be sure to keep all bills relating to treatment, medication and other expenses.

Superswitch's Model 6002 intruder alarm is so small and lightweight that it can be carried with you and used to protect valuable equipment on your travels.

Green card

If you plan to take your car abroad, let your insurance company know. Some automatically provide comprehensive cover throughout the EC to people with fully comprehensive policies. Others will require a small additional payment to cover you. Ask your insurer for a Green Card – whilst this is no longer a legal requirement it can avoid problems in certain EC countries.

To avoid unnecessary delays, take out breakdown cover before you travel, available from most motoring organisations. Some insurance companies include European breakdown cover in their motor insurance policies. Emergency repairs abroad, plus the cost of hiring a replacement car, can add up to a very expensive holiday.

Travel wisely, be prepared to avoid dangerous neighbourhoods

TRAVELLING
WATCHPOINTS

1	**Avoid taking items of real value with you**.
2	Write out a **list of what you are carrying**.
3	Keep **valuable equipment** in your **hand luggage**, along with a few essentials.
4	Avoid attaching your **home address** to the **outside** of your luggage.
5	Make use of **safe deposit** facilities in hotels.
6	**Never leave packed luggage unattended**.
7	Find out **as much as possible** about your destination. Ask the travel agent or courier for **areas to be avoided**.
8	Try to **'blend in'**, and make sure you **know your route in advance**.
9	Always choose a **busy, safe place to ask directions**.
10	Carry **travellers' cheques** and **credit cards**, and **limit cash to a minimum**. Carry it in a money belt.

Chapter 5

Vehicle Security Cars

The statistics

The majority of car thieves are young people. According to one study, most begin in their early to mid-teens, aided by more experienced youths. They do it out of boredom, for the excitement and, eventually, for the money. Over a third of the car thieves questioned went on to stealing cars to order.

Official figures show there are 1.5 million thefts of and from vehicles in the UK, although an independent report puts this figure much higher, claiming that 4 million drivers in Britain had had a car broken into and items stolen over the previous two years. This still means that more than a third of all reported offences are vehicle related.

On the other hand, an NOP poll revealed that 30% of motorists didn't do more to protect their cars because of the expense, while 18% put it down to apathy. Seventy-five per cent said that they might well leave their car unlocked in a petrol station while paying for petrol, and a further 24% admitted they might leave it unlocked when they popped into a shop.

Over 8% said they had left their car unlocked in a public car park within the last month, little realising that 20% of all car crime (up to 40% in some areas) takes place in car parks. Nevertheless, 63% said that security was 'very important' when choosing a car.

With the revision in Group insurance ratings (there are now 20 compared to nine previously) and the publication of the Thatcham Report, which specifies the levels of security a manufacturer must achieve before a car is allocated a particular rating, there is considerable pressure on manufacturers to ensure that premiums are kept down.

Naturally, if a premium is too high for the type of car and its intended market, it is likely that the manufacturer will sell less of that model. Standard equipment now includes high security door locks, alarms and immobiliser systems, glass etching, coded audio equipment, locks for alloy wheels and visible Vehicle Identification Numbers (VIN).

Keeping valuables

Car radio manufacturers have had to fight to keep ahead of the ICE (in-car entertainment) thief. As a result, security coded radios, removable radios and removable radio fascias have been introduced. There are also lockable protective steel housings which can be fitted over the radio to conceal and protect it. Removing it completely is, of course, the most effective method.

Car radios have now been replaced as the top target by mobile telephones. It is the cellphone makers who are concerned to make their phones less attractive to steal. Counter-measures include invisibly marking the phone and a registration system.

In 1993, mobile phone thefts were running at around 10,000 a month and the Metropolitan Police indicated that over 40% of car break-ins within Greater London were related to such

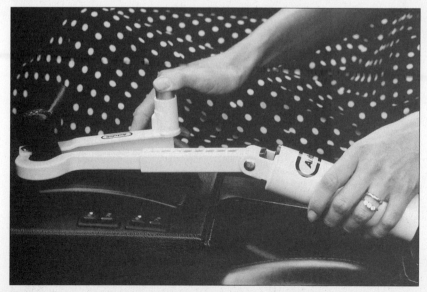

Use a visible deterrent like this device from Autolok which secures the handbrake and gear lever.

thefts. The thieves use the stolen phones for 'cloning' (rechipping so that an unsuspecting customer receives a bill for air-time he or she did not use) or for resale, where they are rechipped to reconnect them to a network.

Choose wisely

How do you know how effective an automobile product is? Initiated by Northumbria police, an organisation called Sold Secure PACT is now spreading nationwide via the police forces. It is a network of installers and retailers who are able to sell and fit tried and tested products which can then be used to help police trace any stolen vehicle fitted with a recognised product.

A technical committee assesses the product, such as an alarm or lock, and will only recognise products that are able to withstand a criminal attack for five minutes, a time scale arrived at from police working knowledge of how long a thief is prepared to work on stealing a vehicle.

The issue of a certificate for each product fitted in accordance with specifications allows the police to set up a database for tracing if ever necessary.

There is also a British Standard for vehicle alarms - BS6803 Part 2 - which establishes a code of practice for systems installed after vehicle marketing. This covers components and installation of an alarm. If you have an alarm installed, make sure the fitter complies with this standard.

AU209 is a standard covering other aspects of vehicle security, including locking systems, security etching and marking of car hi-fi equipment. It may well include the use of laminated glass in cars. A section on immobilisers is also in preparation.

There are many initiatives up and down the country fighting car crime. Vehicle Watch allows the police to identify cars on the road at unusual times. (Check whether your police force operates a scheme like this.) Look, too, for car parks that have a Secured Car Parks gold or silver award. These will have built-in security, such as closed circuit television, regular patrols and good lighting.

However, it is only by thinking twice before we leave our vehicles that we can ensure we don't become another statistic.

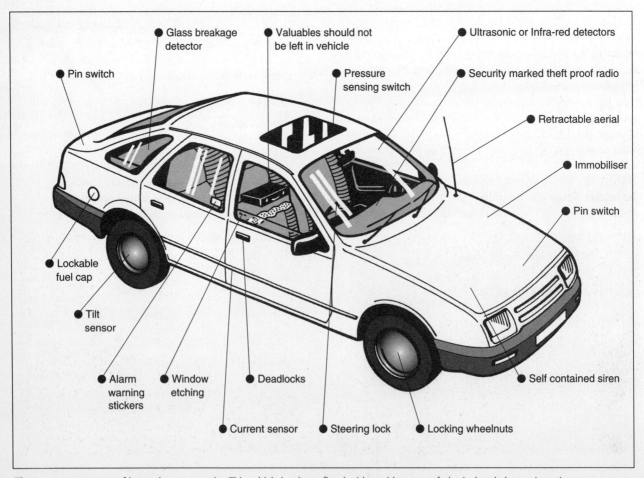

There are many means of improving car security. This vehicle has been fitted with a wide range of physical and electronic options.

Beat the car thief

Eight out of ten car thieves are opportunists, using a few simple tools and very little skill. Often, all it takes is the opening of an unlocked door or reaching in through an open window.

By increasing the time it takes to break into your vehicle, simple security devices can go a long way towards safeguarding your car and its contents. But it's important not to make your car an attractive target in the first place.

Take desirable items with you or lock them away in the boot. If you own an estate car, make or buy a load cover for the luggage compartment. Never leave vehicle documents, cash or credit cards in your car.

Keep your car locked at all times – even when you are at the petrol station. Always take the keys with you and close the windows. It only takes a few seconds to reach in and make off with your camera or wallet.

Make sure, too, that the steering wheel lock is engaged, otherwise the lock could be smashed by a thief forcing the steering wheel. On older cars you can immobilise the vehicle fairly easily by removing the rotor arm.

Research shows 75% of car buyers are prepared to pay for built-in anti-theft features but it is not just new cars which are targets for the thief. Older cars may rely on the owner fitting secondary security – which many owners seem reluctant to spend money on. In many instances, it is these cars which are most at risk.

At the end of the day, any car without some sort of security measure is a target. It may be taken by so-called joyriders, or broken into for a radio or items left in view. With the new MoT regulations, there is even a market for stolen windscreens.

There is a wide range of physical security devices on the market which require little in the way of installation skills, and offer good visible deterrent value. Included amongst the visible deterrents are hook locks linked between the steering wheel and the brake pedal, the steering bar that locks on to the steering wheel to prevent it being turned, locks which fit over the handbrake lever to prevent it being released, and the locking bar that immobilises the gearstick and handbrake. All these devices may be carried in the car and easily locked into place when you leave the vehicle.

Another device, which requires professional installation, is bolted to the vehicle floor and incorporates a high security padlock, operated by a registered key, which is secured around the gear lever in neutral position, to prevent the car being driven away.

Other physical security devices protect individual items fitted to the car. For example, petrol locking caps, locking wheel nuts to protect expensive alloy wheels, wheel clamps and lockable covers which fit over the stereo system.

Most car audio manufacturers are also taking steps to improve security, with stereos which will only operate when a unique code, known only to the driver, is keyed in if the power is disconnected, and radios which can be removed and carried with you.

If you must leave valuables in the car, there are vehicle safes which are bolted to the vehicle floor to protect pull-out stereos, car phones and other items.

Locking up

Locks fitted to older cars are particularly vulnerable and easily overcome, even by less experienced car thieves. Additional or replacement deadlocks, or a central locking system, can be fitted to overcome weak locking devices. There are suitable locks available for DIY fitting but those who prefer a professional installation should contact a local garage or auto-security specialist.

Have all windows etched with the registration number

The Gearlock from Euro Mul-T-Lock is bolted to the vehicle floor and incorporates a high security padlock secured around the gear lever.

Lockable covers are available which protect the car radio. This one is from Arjan.

– etching pens and stencils are available to do this yourself - but for a more professional finish, contact a company which uses a sandblasting technique, or ask your local police if they are planning to organise a property marking day when vehicle windows and contents can be marked.

Alternatively, windows and headlamps can be professionally marked with a unique Security Protection Number (SPN), which is kept on a confidential database, enabling a prospective purchaser, or the police, to check ownership and/or mileage within minutes.

Vehicle Watch

Vehicle Watch is a relatively new scheme set up by police forces, in an increasing number of counties, in a bid to combat vehicle theft on a local level. Members of the scheme – i.e. car owners – display stickers in front and rear windscreens which indicate the times when the vehicle is likely to be on the road.

For instance, cars which are not normally driven at night might display yellow stickers. By displaying these discs, the motorist invites police patrols to stop the vehicle if it is found on the road between midnight and 5 a.m. and check that the driver is the owner of the vehicle or someone authorised by the owner.

Immobilisers

Immobilisers are designed simply to prevent someone from stealing your vehicle. They will not sound an alarm, nor protect the contents of your vehicle. So they should form part of, or supplement, a vehicle alarm system – most are easily linked to compatible systems.

There are many available on the market ranging from basic systems to more sophisticated designs which incorporate dummy cut-out circuits to confuse the thief, or will immobilise the vehicle 30 seconds after the engine stops, even if the key is not removed from the ignition.

Vehicle alarms

Today's vehicle alarms are more sophisticated than the early types and, if properly installed, should not cause false alarms. These were often caused by shock sensors, designed to detect violent movement or attack, reacting to gusting wind or passing cars. More sophisticated movement detectors have made modern systems less prone to false alarms.

Vehicle alarms vary considerably in price, from £50 for a DIY system right up to £1,000 or more for a sophisticated, professionally installed alarm. Before you buy, look for the British Standard – BS6803.

The simplest type of alarm offers ignition cut-out linked to the car's horn or, preferably, a separate siren which is less vulnerable and can be hidden away. Operation may be via an exterior key or a 'hidden' switch inside the vehicle. They offer minimal protection so you would be well advised to install a system offering greater protection than this.

An alarm ought to cut out the ignition but also incorporate devices that will detect attempted entry to the vehicle. This may be done by detecting a drop in voltage or change in current, with the alarm sounding if the car's door, boot or bonnet courtesy lights are operated or there is a change in electrical load. (Make sure that the alarm allows for the vehicle's electric cooling fan to cut in without activating the siren.)

Pressure sensing switches activate the alarm when a drop in pressure inside the vehicle is detected – when a door, window or sunroof is opened, for example. Depending on its sophistication, your alarm may also offer ultrasonic detection or, with DIY kits, this may be an optional extra. Ultrasonic modules emit sonic waves inside the car which, if disturbed by movement, will trigger the siren. Microphones are also offered with some systems, activated by the frequency of noises produced by a forced entry.

For convertibles, where ultrasonic protection would not be appropriate, alternative detection methods, such as infra-red detectors or microwave sensors, may be used. In addition to one or more of these sensing devices, the alarm may incorporate a back-up battery so it will continue to operate, even if the car's own wiring is interfered with. The alarm may also be linked to the headlamps or hazard warning lights to provide visual indication that the alarm has been activated.

Locking wheel nuts are widely available from motor accessory stores.

To deter thieves, opt for an alarm which incorporates a small flashing light mounted to the windscreen or dashboard to indicate that the alarm is in operation, and apply warning stickers to windows to draw attention to the alarm.

Alarms can be armed in a variety of ways. The most basic requires the setting of a switch situated in the car or, less frequently in modern systems, via an exterior key switch. For the forgetful motorist, there are 'passive' alarms which activate automatically a short time after the ignition has been switched off.

A popular method these days incorporates a radio transmitter key fob which activates the alarm remotely. However, scanners can now be used which 'capture' the correct code when it is transmitted by the unsuspecting driver. Some cheap alarms can be 'cracked' in this way. Manufacturers are responding by incorporating anti-scan and anti-grab features into their vehicle alarms.

Modern professionally-installed alarm systems are becoming increasingly sophisticated. Options available range from a 'panic' device which, operated from a remote key fob or a switch in the car, is designed to sound the alarm in order to summon help should you or the car be attacked, right up to an 'anti hi-jack' facility. This enables the thief to drive a short distance before the engine cuts out and the alarm sounds. Security systems can also be linked in to central locking circuits and electrically-operated windows and sunroofs, locking them automatically when the alarm is armed.

Fitting a car alarm system

Although car alarm systems are a better DIY proposition than they ever have been, it's not worth having a go yourself unless you are totally confident. Ask the shop assistant to show you the bits inside the box and the fitting instructions. It will give you an idea of the amount of work required, and the scope of the instructions.

One good example of a sophisticated DIY alarm has an excellent line up of features and even includes a how-to-fit video tape, making it much easier to get things right. Typical cost is around £120 or, professionally fitted, about £30 extra. If you do decide to pay the extra cash, it is the installer's problem if something goes wrong.

What can you expect for your money? At the basic level, you get an alarm which only needs a few simple connections and it will work very efficiently. If you wish to go further, you can connect extra wires for 'interior light turn-on' when the alarm is disarmed. It may also be set up with or without auto-arming and voltage drop sensing.

An alarm with voltage-drop sensing will react to the current draw of a boot light. In other words, it is not necessary to run a wire to a boot pin switch (although this has the advantage on some alarms of tripping instantly). On the other hand, if the battery starts to loose its charge, there's a good chance of a false alarm.

Alarms can often be foiled by forcing the bonnet and snipping wires. This can be combated most effectively by a self-contained siren unit with its own battery.

Cheaper systems without batteries can be made more effective by bolting the siren securely in a position where it is hard to get at the wiring (either from above or below), and taping all alarm wiring onto existing looms. Also, make sure that the battery terminals are securely tightened.

Alarms generally seem more reliable than they used to be. Any trouble you may have will be down to the quality of installation or adjustment. Two of the biggest sources of trouble experienced in this area are using a 'voltage drop' trigger system and setting too much sensitivity on an ultrasonic detector.

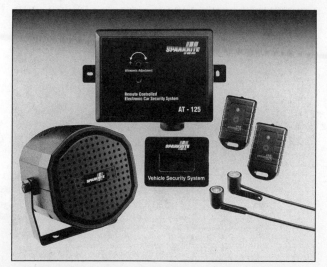

Suitable for DIY installation, the AT125 Remote Control Car Alarm from Sparkrite includes ultrasonic sensors, engine immobilisation, separate siren and a windscreen receiver with armed warning light.

Fitting a car alarm system

Car alarm systems are a better DIY proposition than ever before but it is not a job to tackle unless you are fully confident. Check out the system and its instructions with the shop assistant before you buy. It will give you a rough idea of the type of work required and the scope and competence of the instructions.

Vehicle alarms vary considerably in price, from £50 for a DIY system right up to £1,000 or more for a highly sophisticated, professionally installed alarm. Before you buy, look for the British Standard – BS6803.

At the basic level, Code-Alarm's Anes 75 'Cop in a Box' only needs a few simple connections to work very efficiently. If you go on, other options include setting it up with or without auto-arming and voltage drop sensing.

TOOLS AND MATERIALS

- [ ] Right-angle drill + bits
- [ ] Wire strippers
- [ ] Screwdrivers (various)
- [ ] 12v test lamp
- [ ] Soldering iron
- [ ] Solder
- [ ] Insulating tape

Code-Alarm's Anes 75 'Cop in a box' is a sophisticated DIY alarm with an excellent line up of features, including a how-to-fit video tape.

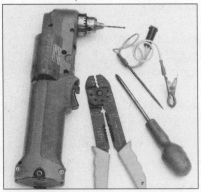

1 Most DIY alarms only require simple tools, apart from some installations requiring a right-angle drill or an adaptor for a conventional type. A simple 12V test lamp will be needed.

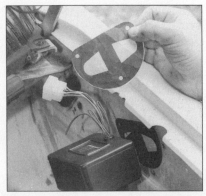

2 The first action is to check the siting of the unit. It should be away from manifold heat, face down to prevent water collecting, and be high enough to be out of reach from under the car.

3 A template is supplied with the Anes to simplify the drilling of the holes for the mounting plate. Always check behind the panel before drilling to avoid piercing wires or brake pipes.

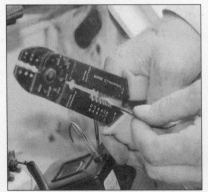

4 Some wires can now be prepared for eyelet terminals, such as the earth wire which can be fastened under one of the bracket mounting screws. Use a star washer to maintain a good contact.

5 A piece of stiff wire can be used as a 'mouse' to pull the wires that need to go through into the car, such as the interior light-sensing wire and the leads to the 'armed' warning light.

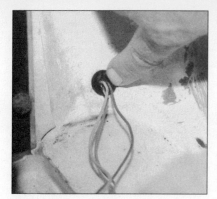

6 The wiring can either be pulled through an existing loom grommet or a new hole could be made (check behind!). Always use a grommet sealed with mastic to keep out water.

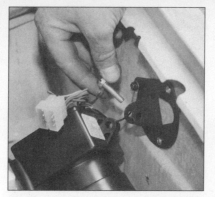

7 The wire threading operation through the bulkhead had to be completed before we could fit the siren unit to its bracket. Mounting must be solid to allow shock sensor to work properly.

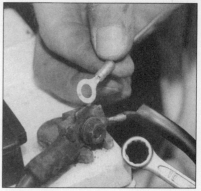

8 Never complete the circuit with the power lead fuse fitted – this is the last item. The eye terminal can be fitted to the battery, though. Try to keep it tucked in with the other wires.

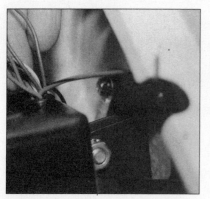

9 The Code-Alarm has options for auto-arming and voltage-drop sensing. To reduce the chance of false alarms, the option loop can be cut if the alarm is connected to interior light circuit.

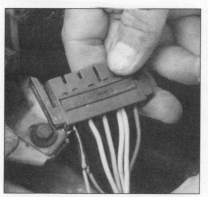

10 The parking or indicator light circuit (depending on the type of alarm) is found using a test bulb to trace the live circuit. An alarm wire is connected to flash lights on arming/disarming.

11 The Code-Alarm is supplied with a heavy duty relay to immobilise the vehicle's starter circuit. We drilled a mounting hole under the bonnet but it can be mounted near the ignition key. Check behind panel before drilling.

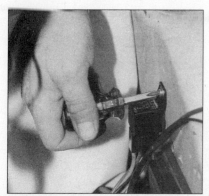

12 Mount the relay away from heat and spray. The starter trigger wire should not be confused with the heavy gauge main cable to the starter.

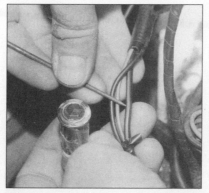

13 The starter trigger wire can be located by earthing the test lamp and probing the insulation with a sharp point. It should only light while the engine is being turned.

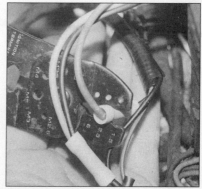

14 The starter wire can be cut and the relay leads spliced in, using crimping butt connectors. A high current flows when starting, so keep the leads as short as possible for reliability.

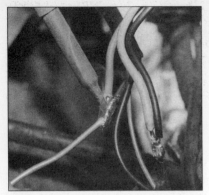

15 If you are confident with a soldering iron, soldered joints are preferable to crimping. The starter wire joint can then be wrapped in insulating tape, making it difficult to find.

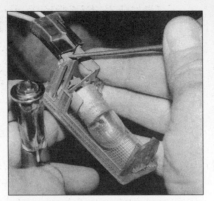

16 Inside the car, the interior light wire is usually easy to trace and can be bulb-tested to check polarity. The Code-Alarm will connect to either polarity – always check instructions here.

17 The arming warning light can also be wired to earth or live, depending on the type of alarm. Most warning lights are a push fit into a single hole. Ours was fitted to the top of...

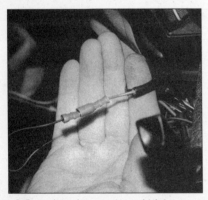

18 ...the column casing, which is a convenient spot, and earthed to a nearby switch-retaining screw. Where the casing is removable, it is a good idea to provide connector termination.

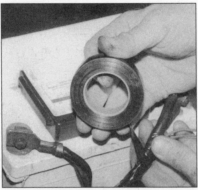

19 Once the wiring is complete and tested, it can be taped up generously, preferably with matching loom tape, to make it difficult to get to the alarm leads and fuses.

20 Part of the checking procedure will, in some cases, involve the self-programming of the remote controls. The Code-Alarm can also be remotely set up for shock sensor sensitivity.

Choosing your system

When choosing an alarm system, consider your options carefully and look around at what is on offer. Visit motor accessory centres, if you are keen on installing your own system , and auto-electricians or specialist alarm installers to find out what is on the market and whether you may be able to install a more sophisticated system yourself.

Pick a system that suits your car and yourself, and consider what you carry in the car and even where it is parked regularly. If yours is a sophisticated radio, you will probably want an alarm that offers internal ultra-sonic protection. If you live in a noisy area, you will need an alarm with a loud siren, and which operates the hazard warning lights.

Take your time - it may even be worth contacting a few insurance companies as some are now teaming up with alarm manufacturers to offer substantial discounts on equipment to policyholders wishing to protect their vehicles.

VEHICLE
WATCHPOINTS

1 **NEVER leave keys in the ignition**.

2 **Always lock all doors** and **close the windows**.

3 **Never leave** your vehicle **documents** in the car.

4 **Lock all valuables out of sight**, or carry them with you.

5 Try to park in **well-lit, well-populated car parks**. Look for a **Secured Car Park** logo for greater peace of mind.

6 In car parks where you pay on the way out, **take tickets with you** to prevent a thief driving away.

7 Always make sure the **steering wheel lock** is **engaged** when you park.

8 Fit a **security device** to the **car stereo**, or buy one you can remove and take with you.

9 **Install an alarm and an immobiliser**.

10 **Security mark all windows** and contents, such as **car stereos** and **mobile phones**.

Pagers

Pagers which alert you when your car is tampered with, or if the car phone rings, are another option. These should, however, be viewed as additions to alarm/immobiliser systems. Some are supplied with a siren, while others offer a siren is an optional extra. Pagers are limited in range, with manufacturers' claims of from 75m (25') up to 2,000m (660').

A new system, introduced from the United States, enables police to track stolen vehicles. Vehicles are fitted with a hidden electronic homing device programmed with a unique code number. If your car is stolen, you simply report it to the police, with the code number.

The police computer then switches on your car's tracking device which emits a radio signal inaudible to the thief but which allows specially equipped police cars to trace your car. Systems currently available include one available to all motorists through the AA.

Tips for two-wheelers

In the UK, a motorcycle is stolen every seven minutes, often for spare parts or resale. Simple precautions can help – park in well-lit, busy places, never leave any valuables behind, and take your helmet with you. Cycles may be secured with a top quality chain and padlock or large 'D-ring'-type high security padlocks.

Fit an electronic immobiliser, or a concealed cut-out switch that breaks any of the low-tension wires to the coil, or simply remove the coil wire.

To tackle the rise in theft, the motorcycle industry is supporting an inexpensive tagging system to help police trace stolen bikes and to deter thieves. It uses coded electronic implants which remain passive until activated by police scanners.

A pack of transponders and DIY fitting instructions are available through motorcycle dealers. Tags are glued in concealed positions and injected into soft components such as seats to make them difficult to find. A thief, therefore, can never be sure whether a motorcycle has been 'tagged'. The police are supplied with scanners to locate tags and can check ownership by contacting a central database.

Alarms are also available, including remote controlled alarm systems specifically for motorcycles, scooters and mopeds. DIY systems incorporate a built-in alarm, adjustable shock sensor and remote panic facility; those with higher specifications are intended for professional installation.

Bikes, Boats & Caravans

The theft of bicycles, caravans, boats and their contents is big business. They are, after all, extremely vulnerable. They're portable, valuable and, left unattended for weeks on end, present an easy target.

If you saw somebody on a garage drive, hitching a caravan up to a car in the early hours, you would probably never suspect that it was being stolen. Similarly, with someone at a lake or riverside, mounting a boat on to a trailer and towing it away.

Even so, leisure equipment can be protected by using common-sense and simple security devices.

General advice

The object is to divert the thief to an easier target. The more obstacles you put in his way, the longer it takes him to steal your boat or caravan and the greater his risk of being observed.

All property should be security marked, with your postcode and the number or first two letters of the name of your house. (See Chapter 2.)

Maintain an up-to-date description and inventory of the contents of your boat or caravan and keep it in a safe place. To help the police, you should record details such as the make, length, colour of your boat or caravan and, in the case of the former, type – such as sail, cruiser, inboard, outboard, etc. The inventory should include all valuable equipment, with details of the manufacturer,

A machine is stolen every seven minutes, frequently for spare parts or resale.

The theft of bicycles, caravans, boats and their contents is big business these days.

brand name, model and serial number, description, value and the location of any security marking. A photographic record might also prove helpful.

For the protection of caravans, the National Caravan Council has devised CRIS – Caravan Registration and Identification Scheme. Under the scheme, every tourer produced from 1992 is visibly marked on the main chassis and up to ten windows with a unique identity code called Vehicle Identification Number (VIN). The 17-character VIN gives precise information about the tourer, including the country of origin, the manufacturer, the National Caravan Council identification code and the year of manufacture.

The VIN and other details of the tourer are recorded on a 'Touring Caravan Registration Document', which is sent to the registered keeper by CRIS and must be kept in a safe place – not in the caravan. All details are then held on a central computer to enable owners of stolen or abandoned tourers to be traced. Details of further dealer or private sales can then be registered on the computer.

When unattended, valuable equipment should be hidden or, better still, locked away out of sight. You may even want to consider installing a safe, but make sure that the floor or walls would provide a secure fixing, and try to mount the safe somewhere out of sight. In the case of boats, bear in mind that there is always the possibility of corrosion.

Make expensive equipment more difficult to steal by bolting things in place and burring over the threads to prevent removal with a spanner. If the boat or caravan is to be left unattended for long periods, make sure that, externally, it is well secured, then strip it internally, removing anything that is portable or valuable. Leave all the curtains, cupboards and drawers open to show a thief there is nothing worth breaking in for.

Boats

Boats are particularly vulnerable; with an estimated £60m worth of boats and equipment stolen in the UK each year, security measures are vital if you are to stay afloat.

Smaller vessels, as well as windsurfers, surfboards and canoes can be locked away out of sight in a well-secured garage – and, again, should be security marked with your postcode.

Larger boats, however, are often kept in their owners' gardens or driveways. Mounted on a trailer, it is simplicity itself for a thief to hitch your boat up to his vehicle and drive away in seconds.

Your main priority must be to ensure that your trailer cannot be towed away. This is achieved very simply by using a dummy ball, which fits into the hitching socket and locks in place, or a hitch lock, which slips over the hitch socket and again is locked in place. These padlocking devices must be sturdy – don't stint on quality.

Other devices which prevent towing include the wheel clamp which, though bulky, provides a strong visual and physical deterrent, and will take considerable time to remove. You could also remove a wheel – an effective but inconvenient deterrent.

One of the most convenient ways to secure boats in your garden or driveway is to install an anchor post. Bolted or cemented into the ground, these can be locked in place and can only be removed by the key holder.

Some thieves are bold enough to remove small boats, boards and canoes from roof racks, if the owners don't secure them properly. Use chains and padlocks to improve security but, to be really safe, avoid leaving equipment unattended.

If possible, remove outboard motors and lock them away

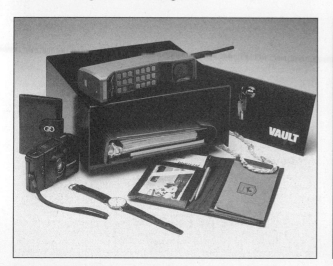

Valuable equipment can be locked away in a safe like the Vault 'X' from Automobile Inparts.

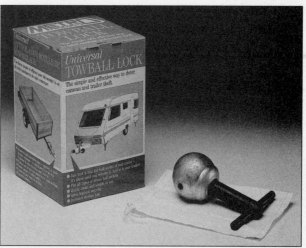

This towball lock from Metro Products locks into the ball socket of a trailer to prevent towing.

safely. If the outboard is difficult to remove, the engine must be bolted firmly in place. Special locks which shroud the securing nuts are available from marine centres.

Motor-powered vessels can be immobilised by interrupting the supply of power to the engines. This is done by removing the distributor's coil wire, preventing the motor from starting. Alternatively, a keyed battery switch can be installed, which prohibits anyone other than the key holder from accessing the vessel's battery power.

Keel boats are particularly susceptible because, even if the engine is immobilised, a thief could still sail away. With both dinghies and keel boats, spare sails should be stowed away safely in a locker and foresails reeled in. For greater security, the boom could be chained to a deck fitting. Other options include removing the tiller or securing the steering wheel with a chain and padlock. Make sure you are adequately insured for the boat and its contents.

Standard door and window locks can be fitted to provide additional security, but an intruder alarm may provide the best protection; contact a marine or specialist boating shop for advice. Make sure that any alarm is unaffected by exterior movement – the last thing you want is an alarm that is activated by river currents or tide change.

The system will probably consist of a control panel – which should be water and shock-proof – a siren and a range of sensors designed for marine use. The sensors should include surface and flush-mount sensors to protect doors, windows and hatches, and others to protect the boat while it is moored, or to protect the outboard motor, and instrument sensors to protect expensive on-board marine instruments.

By adding a strobe light, you can increase the likelihood of your siren being recognised and acknowledged. Smoke, gas and water detectors are also wise investments.

If your boat is moored at a marina, an intruder alarm can often be linked via radio to the marina office or a central station to provide 24-hour protection.

Tagging systems have also been introduced for marine security. Tags, incorporating a unique identification number, are placed on a vessel in two or three locations, or injected into the glass fibre hull. The vessel and registered keeper are then logged on to a central computer database which can be accessed by harbour and river police, Customs and Excise and other approved groups.

These approved organisations are issued with scanners which, from certain distances, are able to read the tag and ascertain ownership. This tagging system is proving very valuable for the security of personal watercraft (jet-skis), and new craft, from 1993 onwards, are sold with these tagging systems already fitted.

DIY tagging kits are easy to install and reasonably priced at under £60 – including the kit and a year's free membership to the Personal Watercraft Association (PWA). Owners of tagged craft are also entitled to reduced insurance premiums. If the craft is sold on, the new owner can obtain a re-registration form and re-register for only £5.

To improve security at marinas and on rivers, some police forces are working with boat owners to set up Boat Watch schemes – run along similar lines to Neighbourhood Watch. Generally speaking, boat owners are encouraged to watch out for each other's vessels and report any suspicious activity to the police, to mark property and generally become more security-conscious.

Choose your marina carefully, with security an uppermost consideration. Ask the management what security measures they offer and check the marina's reputation for security with fellow boat owners. Ideally,

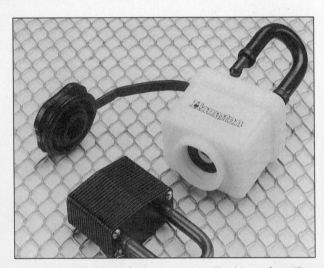

Use waterproof padlocks for marine security, like this one from Eliza Tinsley & Co.

Wheelclamps, like this one from Lionweld Kennedy, provide a strong physical and visual deterrent.

there should be a security guard at the premises. Check, too, whether public access to the boats is limited. If your boat is stored in a compound, make sure the area is well-protected by good fencing and is well-lit at night.

Caravans

Caravans spend much of their life on the owner's front drive or in a compound. Like boat trailers, they need to be immobilised to prevent theft. Hitch locks, dummy balls, wheel clamps and anchor posts, available from caravan and motor accessory shops, will all provide good protection against unauthorised towing.

The National Caravan Council recommends heavy duty 3mm (⅛") thick steel wheel clamps are used, preferably hardened with a built-in high security enclosed lock. The clamp must encompass the tyre and project into the wheel well, covering at least one of the wheel nuts to prevent removal of the clamp by tyre deflation – this level of security may be a condition under some insurance policies. When not in use, the caravan wheels may be removed and stored securely away from the caravan.

Wheels and tyres can also be protected with locking wheel nuts, and there are also devices available which prevent the caravan stays from being raised. Fitted to the two rear stays, these make towing the caravan virtually impossible. Another low-cost method of immobilising the van is to drill a hole in the chassis, close to a wheel and thread a length of plastic-covered chain through the chassis and wheel and secure it with a padlock.

When you are touring, the contents of the caravan can be protected with an alarm system. Battery-operated alarms normally using passive infra-red detection can protect the interior but these often rely on an internal siren, which may not be heard if the caravan is situated at some distance from passers-by.

Some, however, can be linked to an external siren for greater protection. DIY alarms are also available from caravan centres and normally provide a control unit, a waterproof, tamper proof siren for external siting, magnetic contacts and vibration sensors that detect any movement inside the caravan, or of the caravan itself. Alarms may be powered using rechargeable batteries, or the car battery when touring.

One alarm is based on a small electronic safe bolted to the frame of the caravan, which communicates with various sensors via radio signals. Control of the sensors and operation of the safe is achieved through a touch-key pad fitted to the front of the safe. The system may be linked to an external siren or light to alert site security or passers-by to an intrusion. Central monitoring is also available via the site office or, if a telephone line is available, a national security monitoring centre.

On some sites, sophisticated systems detect unwanted visitors. Other sites may employ man-and-dog patrols or install closed circuit television. Sites which provide mains electricity hook-up points can accept caravans fitted with mains-operated intruder alarms.

Caravans should be alarmed and immobilised even when left for only short periods. Time switches can be fitted to lights to give the impression that the caravan is occupied after dark.

If the caravan is not kept at home, it should be stored in a securely locked and alarmed building or in a properly fenced, well-lit, patrolled and securely-locked storage compound – again a requirement under some insurance policies.

Being left unattended for long periods of time, static caravans are just as vulnerable. They should be immobilised and alarmed in much the same way, with curtains open and cupboards and drawers empty and open to deter thieves. Like Boat Watch schemes, some caravan owners have got together to form Caravan Watch on sites around the country.

Motor caravans can be immobilised by removing the engine's rotor arm, fitted to the distributor; by removing a couple of spark plug leads; or by fitting a simple immobilising switch (usually under the dashboard), which prevents electrical current from reaching the coil or distributor. Better still, fit a vehicle alarm with additional sensors to protect the interior of the vehicle.

Fire protection

Modern caravans should be manufactured to meet stringent fire regulations. National Caravan Council member manufacturers and dealers must ensure that new and second-hand caravans are fitted with smoke alarms, manufactured to British Standard 5466. A fire extinguisher is also recommended.

Bicycles

With cycling becoming more popular, and bicycles becoming more sophisticated and expensive, they are a popular target with thieves. Nearly a quarter of a million bicycles are stolen each year and, of the small percentage that are recovered, most are auctioned because the rightful owners cannot be identified.

There are several simple measures to take to prevent your bike becoming another crime statistic. These days many bicycles are fitted with quick-release saddles and, by removing the saddle whenever you leave your bike, you can ensure that a thief would look very conspicuous trying to ride away. Similarly, most bicycles are fitted with quick-release wheels, so the front wheel can be removed or locked to the frame and back wheel when not in use.

Bicycles should be kept locked up with the best lock you can afford, ideally a 'D'-type shackle lock comprising a loop of solid steel (chains are easier to cut through). Bikes should always be secured to something solid, such as a lamp-post or railings, with the lock attached to both the frame and one of the wheels. Lights and luggage bags should always be removed when the bike is unattended.

With bicycles, security marking provides a means of instant recognition. Your postcode and house number, or first two letters of its name, should be stamped on to the frame in several places and a Coded Cycle sticker attached to warn off potential thieves.

Die stamping can be carried out through the cycle dealer or the police, who often arrange local cycle coding sessions. Even if a thief files down the mark or paints over it, it can still be detected by forensic tests.

If you are buying a second-hand bike, try to ensure it is not a stolen one. Ask for proof of purchase and the bike's handbook, and look out for frame numbers or registration marks that appear to have been tampered with. Also ask questions if it looks as though it has been re-sprayed.

The Home Office has produced a form, available from police crime prevention departments and bicycle shops, on which comprehensive details and a photograph of the bicycle can be kept. If the bicycle does get stolen, the record form can be passed on to police to assist identification.

Bicycles should be kept locked up whenever they are not in use.

Stolen bicycles at Oxford. The police check for security marks but few can be easily identified.

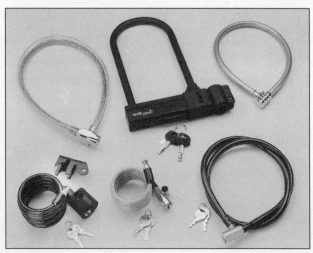

Buy the best bicycle lock you can afford. CeKa offer the Abus range.

LEISURE
WATCHPOINTS

1 **Security mark property**.

2 Maintain an up-to-date **description and inventory** of the contents.

3 Keep valuable equipment **locked away out of sight**.

4 **Bolt expensive, fixed items in place**.

5 When unattended for long periods, secure externally and **strip the boat or caravan internally**.

6 Lock smaller vessels in a well-secured garage.

7 Use **dummy tow balls, hitch locks** or **wheel clamps** to prevent unauthorised towing.

8 Remove **outboard motors** if possible.

9 Bicycles should be **chained to something solid**, and should be **security marked**.

10 Make sure you are **adequately insured**.

Chapter 6

Crime and its prevention
The nature of crime

The statistics on burglary and car crime should make us realise that any one of us is a potential victim, and that we should act now to guard against becoming victims ourselves. Ninety-four per cent of all crime relates to property, and over half are burglaries or vehicle crime. Over 750,000 homes are burgled and over half a million vehicles stolen each year, with almost a million thefts from vehicles.

A recent British Crime Survey, about crimes experienced in the last year, including those that go unreported to the police, estimates that over 15 million crimes were committed (three times the annual levels recorded for equivalent police figures).

Since it is often only the bad news that makes the headlines, it is hard to believe that anyone is doing anything about fighting crime, but much is being done, and many measures that are common-sense and cost little are proving successful.

Returning home to find you have been burgled can be a devastating experience.

Neighbourhood Watch, with 120,000 schemes across the country, shows how local community spirit can work together with councils, police and other bodies not only to react to rising crime but, more importantly, to prevent it happening.

Recent research carried out by West Midlands police, which has an on-going crime pattern analysis system, showed that a house not involved in a Neighbourhood Watch scheme was twice as likely to be broken into as one which did.

Styles of building, both the houses themselves and the layout of estates, are being influenced by schemes such as 'Secured by Design'. Operated in conjunction with builders, whose plans are assessed by police architectural liaison officers, this nationwide scheme was set up in 1988 and includes consideration of landscaping, door and window design and locking, security lighting, alarms and smoke detectors.

The National House-Building Council's requirements have, since 1986, incorporated specific details of security measures to be taken if the house is to receive its 10 year guarantee; some of these have been mandatory since 1989.

All of these contribute to making the homes we live in today and in the future that bit more secure. But there is still much to be done to homes built as recently as the eighties, not to mention those designed centuries ago when doors were comfortably left ajar.

Initiatives and campaigns from the Home Office are helping to change our attitudes, but perhaps the greatest impact will come from the insurance companies, as they continue to mark up premiums each year to match the increasing claims.

Insurers are already having a good deal of influence on car security – not surprisingly as they pay out more than £600 million in theft related claims every year. But it is not just the soaring cost of insurance that should influence us. Fear of crime has proved greater than crime itself.

Reports of violent crime – which actually accounts for less than 300,000 offences per year, one tenth of which were said to be life threatening – tend to be widely reported in the media. While this can be highly distressing, such incidents are in truth few and far between.

We can all protect our elderly and infirm relatives with a little care, attention – and DIY – and, in doing so, reduce their fear. Making sure they don't open the door to strangers, that they look through the door viewer first, and that neighbours or friends call in regularly to see them, are simple precautions to protect and give peace of mind.

Fire prevention and detection is another area which has been addressed by legislation and changing attitudes. The Smoke Detector Bill, introduced in April 1992, makes it mandatory for one or more smoke detectors to be fitted in new homes, and this is echoed in the Building Regulations.

While smoke detectors have to be fitted, by law, in homes in parts of the United States and in Scandinavia, in 1987 only 4% of households in the UK owned a smoke alarm. Now, more than half UK homes have them fitted. Of course, it is important not only to fit these devices but to maintain and use them properly.

Understanding crime

About every 50 seconds, there is a house being burgled somewhere in England and Wales – and one home in 20 is burgled every year.

What we tend to forget in the light of these figures is that many of these break-ins could be avoided and not necessarily by employing expensive, highly sophisticated security measures.

When you consider that, in three out of ten burglaries, a door or window had been left open, you will begin to see how even simple common-sense precautions can play a part in preventing crime. There is a great deal we can do to help ourselves, no matter what our budget.

The burglar

There are many misconceptions about burglars which can lead to an increased fear of crime. Very few burglaries are carried out by professionals – estimates put it at only one in five. The professional burglar has the experience and skill to overcome a reasonable security system and will travel to commit his crime. He is probably part of a network, selling items on to a 'fence' (a receiver of stolen goods), and will take electrical items, jewellery, cash, credit cards and cheque books.

The expert will steal expensive items, such as antiques, and is likely to travel further afield to detached homes in rural areas. He may tour an area looking for a suitable house; then spend time watching the comings and goings of the occupants to gauge when they are most likely to be out.

However, some 80% of break-ins are committed by opportunists – on the look out for an easy target and often acting on impulse. The peak age for offenders is just 15 – some are even younger – and it's likely that he (or she) is based locally, even living on the same housing estate.

A 15-year-old tends to be less mobile, relying on local crime for his income. He knows the area well – which houses are likely to be unoccupied during the day, who owns a dog, etc. He steals cash, to pay bills and buy food, and items for his own use, or which he can pass on to his mates. Many claim that they experience a 'thrill' when they break into houses. By the time they are 30, most burglars have moved on to more sophisticated crime.

The break-in

Two-thirds of burglaries take place during the week, when there is a greater likelihood of the home being unoccupied. The opportunist will look for a house which appears to be unoccupied, and where security is lax – perhaps a window has been left open, or the key has been left in the back door. He may ring the door bell to see whether a dog barks, or if his call is answered. If it is, he can easily make his excuses and move on to a more likely target. If he can break in unseen, so much the better – 64% of burglars gain access at the back or side of properties where the chance of being spotted is less.

The noise and time it takes to break through laminated glass will deter most intruders.

Once inside, the burglar will probably bolt the front door – to warn him if you return home. Then he will look for a quick exit – keys left in or near the front or back door, or patio doors which can be released from inside. If it is easy to get out, it means that larger objects such as electrical items can be removed without difficulty, and he can leave quickly should anyone return home.

To reduce the likelihood of being trapped in a house, a burglar will often start upstairs in the main bedroom, pocketing cash, credit cards and jewellery; checking cupboards, drawers and the pockets of clothing where money may be kept. Once downstairs, he will check the lounge and dining room, emptying drawers and shelves and pocketing small items of value.

If he has an easy exit and transport available, larger items such as hi-fi systems and videos may also be removed. Finally, he may head for the kitchen to search for cash set aside to pay the milkman or window cleaner. He may also check the garage and shed, stealing tools to sell on to friends, or dispose of at a car boot sale. And all this can be achieved in a matter of minutes.

Despite the emotional impact of a burglary and the cost of repairing doors and windows, the value of the property lost may be very small - in 25% of burglaries, the value of property stolen is nil; in 23%, under £100; and in 52% of cases, over £100.

There is only a 5% chance that everything will be recovered. About 86% of victims have nothing returned. Official figures reveal that only one in ten thieves are caught stealing from individuals and taking bicycles, and the detection rate for robberies stands at only 22%. Undoubtedly, prevention is better than cure, but it is very much up to you to take responsibility for your own security – and people need to work in partnership to fight crime in their communities.

Coping with the event

Many people dread returning home to find a burglar in the house, or worse, waking up to find an intruder. But, in the majority of cases, a burglar will try to avoid confrontation. If you do return home and think that someone is inside, do not enter. Go to a neighbour, or the nearest phone box, and call the police immediately.

If you wake in the night and hear an intruder, the police do not recommend that you confront him, or pretend to be asleep. Instead, switch the lights on and make a lot of noise. If you are on your own, pretend there is someone with you and call out to them. Most burglars will leave as soon as they realise they have been heard. Phone the police as soon as it is safe to do so.

While you are waiting for the police to arrive, do not touch anything, as you could destroy vital evidence. You will be asked whether you are immediately aware of any missing items; electrical goods will be the most apparent, and the police officer will need an immediate list to circulate in the hope they can stop someone. Other items may not come to mind until a month or so later.

Clues

If the door has been forced, or glass broken, or if there are jemmy marks, the house may be worth fingerprinting. If the Scenes of Crime Officer is called, you will be told to try to preserve the scene. Don't move anything that might be of assistance, and look out for things that will be needed for fingerprinting.

Any footprints outside should be covered with something that won't spoil the mark. The police will advise you on what should be preserved; you will probably be allowed to tidy up everywhere else.

If you need to carry out emergency repairs, make sure the firm you contact quotes a reasonable price; some take advantage of such situations. Keep receipts for your insurance claim. If cheque books or credit cards have been stolen, inform the issuing company immediately.

It is only after you have dealt with the immediate tasks that you will have time to reflect. You will probably want to improve your security to prevent the same thing happening again, so ask your Crime Prevention Officer to call and advise you on which locks to fit and which other precautions he would recommend.

If the door has been forced it may be worth fingerprinting.

It's always difficult to forget a burglary. You may want to scrub the house clean from top to bottom, redecorate, even move away. But it's important to try to forget it and get life back to normal. Friends and family can help, as well as volunteers from the local Victim Support Scheme.

These volunteers can provide practical advice as well as a shoulder to cry on, reassuring victims that their reaction is perfectly normal. The volunteer may also help you to improve security, carry out repairs, and help out with insurance claims and form filling. Your local police station will be able to put you in touch with your local Victim Support Scheme.

Crime has been increasing all over the western world for most of the past 30 years, with 94% of recorded crime against property. There are several reasons for this - more crime is being reported to the police and, most important, there is an increase in opportunity.

Increasing buying power means more people own more cars and a greater range of portable electrical goods. Add to this the generally inadequate level of security, and it's not surprising that there are so many opportunists earning their living through burglary.

Out of a nationwide sample of 1,300 homes, only 33% had door locks approved to BS3621 – the standard recommended by most British insurers. The same survey found that 29% of householders only had a night latch on the front door (a lock which, on its own, offers very little security), fewer than 25% of homes had more than a basic mortise lock fitted to the front door, and only three in ten homes had bolts on the back door.

Furthermore, less than one-tenth of householders bothered changing the locks when they moved house, meaning that 90% of British householders have no idea who has a key to their home.

The most effective way to fight crime is to deny offenders easy opportunities. Crime prevention measures can and do work. For example, by studying the methods of the most common type of thief – the opportunist – it has been found that he will nearly always opt for the house that is easiest to break into.

Homes with security measures are less likely targets. A review of data from a recent British Crime Survey shows that, in over half of all attempted burglaries where the burglar failed to gain entry, at least three or more security measures had been implemented. The setting up of Neighbourhood Watch schemes has also, in some cases, been shown to reduce burglary and car theft within the immediate neighbourhood.

In partnership against crime

Over recent years a number of initiatives have been set up to fight crime, adopting a partnership approach. The Kirkholt project in Lancashire is one such example. The estate has over 2,000 semi-detached houses and, when the project started in 1986, it had a burglary rate of one in four households broken into every year.

By bringing together local agencies, such as the housing department, police, probation services, the gas and electricity boards and a team of university researchers, the burglary level was dramatically reduced.

The problems were overcome by adopting numerous schemes. Probation officers interviewed 76 recently-convicted burglars to find out what sort of houses they targeted and what might have deterred them. It was found that Rochdale's burglars were not prepared to travel far from home and that signs that a house was unoccupied were of primary importance when choosing a target.

The police provided a full-time local project co-ordinator and, by interviewing all burglary victims and their neighbours, found that 70% of entry points were visible from a neighbour's house. Consequently,

Neighbourhood Watch schemes have been shown to reduce burglary.

neighbours were encouraged to participate in the scheme, keeping an eye out and maintaining signs of occupancy when neighbours were away. This led to the setting up of numerous Home Watch schemes and a 50% reduction in the burglary rate in the first seven months of the project.

This partnership approach led to the government's Five Towns Initiative and then the Safer Cities scheme, which aims to cut crime and lessen the fear of crime in inner city and urban areas by reducing opportunities for crime with better security.

The initiative has concentrated on areas with high crime rates and socio/economic problems, and aims to involve local people in running local multi-agency projects to improve community safety.

Schemes have reported numerous successes: including a housing estate in Keighley where domestic burglaries were reduced initially by 85% as a result of fitting improved window and door locks; a housing estate in Wolverhampton where burglaries were reduced by 40% over three years through a range of target-hardening and social crime prevention measures; the Deptford High Street Business Security scheme which led to a 25% reduction in crime; and a reduction in fear of crime in Sunderland where 97% of the 3,300 elderly people who had security lights and locks fitted to their homes reported feeling much safer as a result.

The 'Secured by Design' initiative mentioned previously reports remarkable achievements. Begun in 1988 as a police initiative in the south-east of England, it covers four main areas – estate design, to create an environment to deter unwelcome intruders by landscaping

and natural surveillance; physical security, including the design of and security requirements for doors and windows; security lighting and smoke detectors; and the installation of integral basic wiring for intruder alarms.

House builders who conform to the 'Secured by Design' minimum security recommendations can display a unique logo which shows purchasers which houses and developments meet police security recommendations. In Sussex, 2,847 homes have been 'Secured by Design', incorporating 65 housing estates and, according to Sgt Peter Hardy of Sussex Crime Prevention Department Design Advisory Service, not one burglary has been reported since the schemes were initiated.

Government crime prevention publicity campaigns have also gone some way in deterring crime. In the first three months of its Car Crime Prevention Year, the Home Office reported a fall of over 2.5% in car crime.

Neighbourhood Watch

Since the launch of the first scheme back in the 1980s, Neighbourhood Watch has played a vital role in the fight against crime. It is a very low cost security measure, yet it can have a great impact on local crime. A scheme in Bristol, for instance, reported a 90% decrease in crime in the three years since their Watch was launched and others in Wythenshawe – reputedly the largest council estate in Europe – reported a fall in house burglaries of almost 21% in only one year.

Certainly, many of the thousands of schemes set up today seem to exist in little other than name only, having little effect on crime. But the success stories prove that Neighbourhood Watch can work – and very effectively. So what exactly is Neighbourhood Watch, and how can you ensure that, should you set up a scheme, it will be effective in fighting crime?

Getting to the roots

Neighbourhood Watch originated in the United States. Citizens of San Francisco were so desperate to reduce high crime rates that they decided to take action. The idea proved so successful that it spread to other American cities suffering from rising crime and violence.

The idea of neighbours banding together to beat crime captured the imagination of the UK population, though inevitably there were reservations. Some people felt that a successful Watch would simply divert burglary to a

Physical security should be given priority.

nearby neighbourhood that had not yet taken steps to protect itself. Others feared it would mean 'vigilante-style' gangs roaming the streets and innocent people having their privacy invaded by well-meaning, if over-enthusiastic, neighbours.

This is not what Neighbourhood Watch (or Home Watch, as it is also called) is about. It is merely about neighbours keeping their eyes and ears open as they go about their daily business, and reporting anything suspicious to the police. Members work together with the assistance of a trained police officer. Under no circumstances are Watch members encouraged to 'have a go' and put themselves at risk in a potentially dangerous situation.

Neighbourhood Watch was introduced to Great Britain in 1982, with the first scheme set up in the Cheshire stock-broker belt village of Mollington, following a spate of burglaries. Within just a few months, the local burglary rate had dropped dramatically, proving that Neighbourhood Watch could be an effective tool in the fight against crime.

As a result, with the support of police forces and the Home Office, Neighbourhood Watch schemes were set up all over the country, with numbers now totalling over 120,000.

Starting a scheme

Setting up a scheme is easy – providing your neighbours are keen on the idea as well. So, before taking the matter further, have a word with some of them and find out how enthusiastic they really are. Then, contact the Crime Prevention Officer at your local police station, who will advise you on setting up the Watch. One of the best ways to augment a scheme is to base it on an existing local community initiative such as a Residents' Association.

A Neighbourhood Watch scheme is not a vigilante force. Members are simply asked to be alert and to note discreetly any suspicious activity. A scheme should also teach members to be more security-conscious. The Crime Prevention Officer may give a talk, show videos or carry out home surveys to teach members how to improve their own home security.

He, or the local beat officer, may also loan security marking kits to the scheme to enable members to mark their valuables, and will also provide literature which explains Neighbourhood Watch, incident report cards and Neighbourhood Watch stickers which members display in their windows to indicate that they are security-conscious.

Neighbourhood Watch areas are also identified by street signs displayed around the area which can be an effective deterrent. Again, the Crime Prevention Officer will be able to advise you on purchasing and erecting these signs.

Organisation

For a scheme to work effectively, it needs some sort of organisation; neighbours need to know who they can contact for advice, how to report suspicious incidents, and to whom. The organisation of a scheme depends largely upon the area in which it is situated. Generally, in residential areas schemes are divided up into small, manageable zones so that each scheme has a well-defined area of the neighbourhood to watch.

One of the neighbours – preferably an enthusiastic, active one who is home all day – is then appointed area co-ordinator. He or she is responsible for regular contact with the police, recruiting and maintaining day-to-day contact with the street co-ordinators, and organising Watch group meetings.

Each street or block of flats within the Watch should have a street co-ordinator, who remains in regular contact

Working together to fight crime.

Neighbourhood Watch or Home Watch street signs indicate that you are security conscious and watching out for suspicious activity.

with their members and who can be contacted easily should any suspicious activity be noted. They in turn contact the police and area co-ordinator. They should also hold regular meetings with their own Watch members, invite newcomers to join the scheme and distribute newsletters and/or other literature.

In most neighbourhoods, there will be some neighbours who don't want to get involved, usually because they are under the false impression that they will have to act as 'snoops' or patrol the streets at night or that it will cost them money!

Because Neighbourhood Watch is community-based, it is best to try to involve everyone. So make sure you know exactly what being a member of a scheme involves so that you can counter such ideas. You could organise a meeting with the Crime Prevention Officer as well to add some weight to your arguments.

If people are adamant that they don't want to join, don't worry. By living in your scheme area they are already involved – and you can look out for their property even if they don't want to play an active role.

When a Neighbourhood Watch scheme is first set up, enthusiasm amongst members is high, with everyone keen to play a role. Meetings will probably be held regularly and be well attended, literature will be distributed promptly, suspicious activity will be reported and, if crime falls in the immediate area, the scheme will be deemed a success.

This is when complacency can set in and crime figures start to creep back up. The secret of a successful Neighbourhood Watch scheme is maintaining this initial level of enthusiasm. This can depend largely on the personality of the co-ordinators. As such, the appointment of these people should not be treated lightly. An enthusiastic and active co-ordinator will ensure that a scheme remains active and that members continue to take an interest in it.

Schemes often fail because members are not kept informed of what's happening. The publication of regular newsletters is vital, keeping members up-to-date with local crime trends and incorporating home security advice. For added impetus, the newsletter can also contain community news, such as local events, births, marriages and anniversaries, fund-raising activities, quizzes, even a page for children.

Meetings should be made interesting to encourage people to attend, with videos and guest speakers organised from the police, fire brigade, security experts, Victim Support scheme or other relevant bodies.

A further incentive is the fact that several major insurance companies offer discounts on home contents insurance to active Neighbourhood Watch schemes. Contact a local broker for more information.

Of course, meetings and newsletters have to be paid for, and schemes have implemented various methods of fund-raising. Some ask members to donate a small sum of money each year to scheme funds, others carry advertising in their newsletter from local businesses, some have secured sponsorship from local companies and others use fund-raising as a way to foster community spirit, with social events held throughout the year.

Some enthusiastic schemes have taken fund-raising a lot further, raising money for local charities, organising outings for Watch members, even raising money to buy locks and alarms for elderly neighbours or to buy their own photocopier, printing press or word processor for publication of their own community magazine or newsletter.

Neighbourhood Watch is not just about fighting crime. Community involvement has re-kindled the old

Some schemes organise activities to raise funds, improve the local area, and foster community spirit.

Watch has rekindled the old community spirit, bringing neighbours together as friends and encouraging them to look out for one another.

community spirit, bringing neighbours together as friends and encouraging them to look out for one another.

Contact is being established with those living alone, Childwatch schemes are ensuring that children are escorted safely to and from school and, perhaps most important, Neighbourhood Watch schemes have reduced the fear of crime which restricts some people's lives.

Activity list

Successful schemes tend to rely on fund-raising schemes and social activities involving Neighbourhood Watch members to maintain enthusiasm and raise funds for charities and/or scheme coffers. Here are a few ideas you might wish to implement:

- Ask local companies if they would like to sponsor your scheme, helping out with photocopying, printing etc.
- Sell advertising in your local newsletter.
- Organise sponsored events, such as litter clean-ups, walks or runs.
- Hold a property marking day with the local police.
- Ask neighbours to donate items for a jumble or car boot sale.
- Organise coffee mornings.
- Involve local children – organise discos or games days or competitions for younger members.
- Ask an appropriate charity whether they would be willing to donate locks or door chains for the local elderly.
- Organise security displays and exhibitions.
- Ask members for a small annual donation.
- Hold dances or amateur theatre evenings.
- Organise outings to the seaside, famous gardens, popular shows etc.
- Hold a barbecue or a safari supper.
- Ask local security firms for a group discount on products.

Above all, make fund raising fun!

The local Crime Prevention or Beat Officer based at the police station will be happy to carry out a free survey for you, and suggest ways of improving your security.

Good advice is available from a specialist security centre.

Getting advice

There are numerous sources of information to help you choose the security devices best suited to your home as well as organisations which will help with any problems or complaints.

One of the best starting points is the local police station, or Neighbourhood Watch scheme. The old Crime Prevention Department is more often called 'Community Liaison' these days, and covers crime prevention issues from home security and car crime to schools, safety of children and other areas of concern.

The Community Liaison Department usually includes a Crime Prevention Officer and a Community Liaison Officer, who will co-ordinate the work of local beat officers and, in some areas, officers allocated especially to Neighbourhood Watch schemes.

They are very approachable and usually willing to provide information in the form of advisory leaflets and product guidance, although they will not officially recommend specific companies or devices.

The Crime Prevention Officer or a specially trained officer will also be able to carry out a free survey of your home, point out the vulnerable areas in need of greater protection and suggest types of product to improve security. They can also supply you with a list of local alarm installers and security stockists.

Shop around…

For more detailed information on products, it is best to shop around. Many large superstores carry a good cross-section of locks, lighting and DIY alarm systems, while specialist security centres or alarm installers will be able to give detailed advice on the products of the type suggested by the police or Neighbourhood Watch adviser.

A good security centre should also be able to offer you a range of door and window locks, safes, security lighting, alarm equipment, access control products, personal alarms, car security, grilles and the fixtures and fittings necessary to complete the job.

They should have the technical ability to advise you on the right product to protect your type of windows, doors and valuables, given the right information (you may need to measure the thickness of the door and know what your windows are made of – wood, UPVC or metal, for example). Products and locations vary greatly, so do make sure fitting instructions are included in the pack. If there aren't any, ask the retailer to suggest the best way of carrying out the installation.

Trade associations

A number of trade associations, to which alarm installers and locksmiths may belong, are also prepared to give advice. Professional associations help reassure you that their members work to certain British Standards, have certain qualifications and that their work is inspected on a regular basis. Associations may also give you some recourse if things go wrong (see our list of useful contacts at the back of this book).

The main association for locksmiths is the Master Locksmiths Association (MLA), who will put you in touch with your nearest MLA members and offer an advisory leaflet 'Guide to Home Protection'. You can write to them for this or call their helpline to locate a reputable locksmith in your area. The MLA runs its own examinations and includes locksmiths and manufacturers as members.

There are rather more associations co-ordinating the activities of alarm installers. The National Approval Council for Security Systems (NACOSS) is a regulatory body with over 500 listed companies. NACOSS recognised firms have to supply accounts for two years of trading and their premises and installations are regularly inspected.

As well as installing to BS4737, these installers must achieve the quality assurance standard BS5750 within two years of gaining NACOSS recognition. NACOSS will send you a list of their approved installers, including information on the association itself and, if you use one of their installers, the company should provide you with a user's handbook If you have cause for complaint, NACOSS will inspect your alarm system free of charge.

Security Services Association (SSA) has about 190 members and recommends that you look carefully at the

Check Yellow Pages for security installers.

qualifications of anyone installing an alarm system for you. They should have at least the National Vocation Qualification (NVQ) or relevant City & Guilds qualifications. SSA members should also supply you with a leaflet explaining the benefits of having an alarm installed by an SSA member, as well as how to complain or ask for help relating to an alarm system.

The association charges a £75 plus VAT inspection fee if there is a problem with a member's alarm system which they are asked to investigate or they will suggest talking to the local Trading Standards Officer who may take up the complaint for you. SSA does not yet have the same influence with insurance companies as NACOSS but a growing number of insurers will accept its members' work and offer insurance accordingly.

The British Security Industry Association (BSIA) includes many of the larger security companies as its members. It has available a free booklet 'The Security Directory' which provides information on each member, as well as describing products offered by the companies, who are often also NACOSS recognised firms.

Many electricians now offer security systems. Some may belong to the Electrical Contractors' Association's (ECA) security division, which requires members to have traded for a minimum of three years, to provide fully audited accounts, and be inspected on a regular basis. The ECA also offers a list of members, will suggest various useful contacts, and has a leaflet on how to choose a security installer.

Crime Concern is very much involved with helping Neighbourhood Watch schemes and has produced a booklet on how to set up a successful scheme. It gives advice on Neighbourhood Watch and suggests suitable contacts for those requiring more information on security matters in general.

Finally, the Association of British Insurers (ABI) produces a wealth of free advisory material on home security and other related subjects, including insurance, safety and vehicle security. To receive any of these please, send them a stamped self-addressed envelope to the address shown at the back of this book.

The design approach

Landscaping of new estates and built-in security, such as better lighting, grass mounds to create visible yet pleasant barriers and thorny bushes to deter intruders are all ideas being used to create a better and more pleasant environment. The 'Secured by Design' scheme has the backing of over 200 developers and, working with police forces, they are designing homes with better layout, door and window design, locking, security lighting, intruder alarms and smoke detectors. Builders are now seeing these factors as giving a home sale value, and where they once left security until the end of a building project, when there was little left in the kitty, they are beginning to budget for such improvements. The National House-Building Council (NHBC) also includes security in the requirements which a builder has to comply with before being able to offer the NHBC ten-year warranty.

So security, whilst it is inevitably associated with crime, is being used to improve the homes we live in, create a better environment and ensure we can feel safer, happier and more secure wherever we are.

Part of Seymour Gate at Chafford Hundred in Essex, a 'Secured by Design' development.

NEIGHBOURHOOD
WATCHPOINTS

1   **Make sure you have the support of neighbours** before attempting to set up a scheme.

2   Contact the **Crime Prevention Officer** at your local police station for advice.

3   Appoint **enthusiastic, active neighbours** as co-ordinators.

4   Display Neighbourhood Watch **street signs** and **window stickers** to deter thieves.

5   Keep members **interested and informed** with **monthly meetings and newsletters**.

6   Organise **social events** to maintain **enthusiasm** and neighbourliness.

7   Ask for **feedback on successes** from the police, and **document local crime statistics**.

8   Maintain **regular contact** with your **local council**, as well as voluntary organisations.

9   Contact **insurance companies** to find out whether they offer **discounts to Watch members**.

Glossary

Access control

Various methods of allowing entry. This could be with a digital lock, mechanical or electronic, a magnetic card, video or audio entry and the latest proximity and hands-free systems which use radio signals to confirm a code.

Biometric – Controlling access using personal characteristics (fingerprints, hand prints, retina patterns etc.)

Fail safe – A locking device that unlocks the door if power fails, and requires continuous power to stay locked.

Fail secure – A locking device that locks the door if power fails and requires power to unlock the door.

Hands-free – Technology which allows a cardholder to gain access without having to actually present a card or enter a code.

Keypad – A non-QWERTY keyboard for inputting codes and information.

Magnetic stripe card – A card with a band of ferrous material that can be magnetically encoded.

PIN (Personal Identification Number) – A code assigned to a cardholder which is entered at the keypad.

Proximity – Technology using radio frequency or inductive principles to stimulate and read cards that transmit unique identification codes.

Stand-alone – An access control system, mains or battery operated, which does not require an additional controller.

Void – To delete a card or code.
(With acknowledgement to Cardkey)

Alarms

Anti hi-jack – On a vehicle security system this enables the car to be immobilised and the alarm sounded after the car has been driven a short distance.

Autodialler (or communicator) – Can be linked to an alarm system to send alert messages to a number of pre-programmed telephone numbers.

Bell box – Houses the external siren for an intruder alarm system. 'Dummy' bell boxes are available as a deterrent.

Central station – A remote location to which signals from the alarm are sent using a variety of methods (telephone line and radio networks, for example) to enable keyholders and emergency services to be contacted when necessary.

Control panel – The heart of the system, able to set, unset, turn zones on and off, process signals from the various devices connected to the system, including, in some panels, identifying faults.

Current sensor – Like the voltage drop sensor, this detects the opening of doors on a vehicle security system.

Detection pattern – Area of volumetric coverage of a detector.

Digital communicator – A device which allows the alarm system to 'pick up' a phone line and dial the central station to raise the alarm.

Exit/entry delay – A part of the alarm system which allows the user or engineer to set the amount of time allowed to enter and exit the premises before the alarm is triggered.

LCD – Liquid crystal display panel which provides a digital readout. Used in alarm and access control systems to display instructions to the user at the panel.

LED – Light emitting diode (often used to indicate alarm status).

Magnetic reed switches – Alarm system detection device fitted to doors and windows. If the door or window is opened the break in the circuit will trigger an alarm.

Microwave detector – A detector that uses microwaves (high frequency radio waves) to detect motion.

Motion detector – Passive infra-red, ultrasonic and microwave sensors.

Panic/Personal attack (PA) button – Alarm activation device which will trigger the alarm even when the control panel is switched off. Should be sited near the front door, or in the main bedroom.

Passive infra-red detector (PIR) – Sends out infra-red beams within its field of detection. Interruption of these beams will activate an alarm system or security lighting.

Personal alarm – A small battery or gas-operated alarm which can be carried in a pocket or handbag.

Pressure sensing devices – Activate an alarm by detecting a drop in air pressure.

Rechargeable self-contained siren module (RSCB) or Self-actuating bell (SAB) – ensures that an alarm siren will continue to sound even if the power is cut or interrupted.

Remote keypad – Where the control panel is hidden away, basic programming of a system is possible from one or more keypads.

Stand-alone alarm – A portable device that can be moved around to protect one room or specific area. Incorporates its own built-in siren and detection device.

Ultrasonic detection – Detects motion by transmitting a high frequency which reflects off objects in an area. If these 'reflections' are changed the detector triggers the alarm.

Vibration detection – A device sensitive to various frequencies (such as breaking glass or vibration).

Voltage drop sensor – Used in a vehicle security system, this detects when a door is opened, or other electrical load imposed.

Wire-free alarms – These utilise radio frequencies to communicate between detectors and control panel, overcoming the need for unsightly wiring.

General

All-risks cover – Insurance for items that are likely to be taken out of the home.

Anti-climb paint – A substance designed to remain sticky for a number of years which is painted on to drainpipes and other surfaces to prevent an intruder climbing to an upper storey.

Casement window – A window that is hinged vertically.

Ceramic markers – Permanently mark china and ceramics by depositing a metallic compound on the surface of the glaze.

Die-stamping – Method of property marking for large metal items using a special set of punches.

Etching – A permanent mark applied to hard surfaces with a hard-tipped engraver, acid or sandblasting technique.

Indemnity – For items insured on an indemnity basis you will be paid the full cost of repairing damaged articles or of replacing stolen or destroyed articles, less an amount for wear, tear and depreciation.

Louvre window – A window with glass fitted in narrow, horizontal slats which are easily removed.

Replacement-as-new – Insurance on this basis means you will be paid the full cost of repairing damaged articles, or the cost of replacing them with equivalent new articles if they are stolen or destroyed.

Security marking – A method of permanently marking property, normally with the postcode, to ensure its safe return.

Ultra-violet ink – 'Invisible' marking which can only be detected under ultra-violet light.

Locks

Automatic deadlatch – A rim lock with a main bolt which automatically locks or is deadlocked when the door is closed.

Bit – The part of the key which is specially shaped or notched to operate the mechanism of its own particular lock.

Blank – A partly made key, ready for cutting.

Cylinder lock – A lock which has its mechanism contained in a cylinder. Made up of pin or disc tumblers and springs.

Deadlock – A lock with only a square ended deadbolt.

Differs – An abbreviation of 'different combinations'.

Dummy ball – A device to protect the towball on caravans or trailers to prevent unauthorised towing.

Hitchlock – Prevents unauthorised towing of a caravan or trailer.

Jamb – The vertical member of a door or window frame.

Lever – A flat-shaped moveable detainer in a lock which provides security and differs.

Master-key – A key which will open any number of locks in a master-keyed system. Locks can be keyed at various levels to open certain doors and not others while one master-key will open them all.

Mortise – A hole cut into the thickness of one edge of a door to accommodate a mortise lock or latch.

Mortise lock – A lock mortised into the stile of a door or window, and key-operated.

Nightlatch – A rim or mortise latch with a bolt which can be withdrawn by key from the outside or by knob or lever handle from the inside. A snib will hold the bolt so the lock remains open and will deadlock the bolt when in the closed position.

Padbolt – Incorporates a bolt which shoots into the surrounding framework and is secured in place with a padlock.

Rim lock – A lock fitted by screwing it to the face of the inside of the door. It will have a rim cylinder on the outside.

Shackle – The shaped loop of a padlock.

Striker or striking plate – A shaped flat metal plate fixed to the door frame or jamb into which the bolts shoot. Used with all mortise locks and some rim locks

Wheelclamp – A device fitted around a car or caravan wheel to prevent towing or driving away.
(With acknowledgement to Yale Security)

Video entry

The facility to see, using a camera and monitor, who is at the door, and often to open the door remotely.

Auto-iris – Automatic method of adjusting iris f stop number.

Camera – A unit containing an imaging device, requiring an optical lens and producing a video signal.

CCTV – Closed circuit television.

Coaxial cable – A specialist cable designed for use with wide bandwidth signals.

Lux – Light levels specified as daylight, lowlight, moonlight and starlight. Infra-red may be used to supplement ambient light.

Video monitor – The picture end of the system. The more lines per inch the better the picture.

British Standards you should know:

BS4737 – In numerous parts relating to various types of alarm, their components, planning and installation, maintenance, records and external alarms. All good installers should comply with this standard.

BS6799 1986 – This is the British Standard Code of practice for wire-free intruder alarm systems which grades complete systems in line with the degree of monitoring they achieve.

Class I requires detectors/devices to transmit an alarm signal and for low battery warning to be given.

Class II should also be able to indicate at the control panel which of the detectors/devices have been triggered.

Class III is for more sophisticated systems which are able to monitor the transmission channels and detect any interference which could jam the signal for over 30 seconds providing a fault indication at the controller.

Class IV & V, as well as fulfilling the requirements of all the other grades, are for higher risk alarm installations and are known as 'supervised' inasmuch as the signals are periodically checked by the system.

Class VI has been approved by the Association of Chief Police Officers and, in meeting their requirements, will be responded to by the police if an alarm is triggered.

BS3621 – The standard for thief resistant locks. Until recently the insurers' byword, but new guidelines have recently been introduced which extend the locks acceptable for insurance purposes.

BS5446 – Look for this standard if you are buying a battery-operated smoke alarm.

BS6707 – Specification for intruder alarm systems for consumer installation. Details components necessary for a kit.

BS5979 – Code of practice for remote monitoring stations.

BS6800 – Specification for home and personal security devices.

BS6803 Part I – The standard for alarm systems installed as original equipment by car manufacturers.

BS6803 Part II – Code of practice for installation of alarm systems in vehicles in the after-market.

BS7150 – Code of practice for intruder alarm systems with mains-wiring communication.

BS8220 Part 1 – Guide for the security of buildings against crime. Good general advice.

BS AU209 – Vehicle security standard in several parts covering locks, in-car entertainment, security marking of glazing, central locking and deadlocking systems.

Useful addresses

Advanced Design Electronics
Dixon Road
Knowsley Industrial Park
North Merseyside L33 7XR
Tel: 0151 549 1550

Aritech UK Ltd
Essex Court, Ashton Road
Harold Hill, Romford
Essex RM3 8UF
Tel: 014023 81496

Secur + Systems
Artistic Ironworkers Supplies Ltd
Edwin Avenue
Hoo Farm Industrial Estate
Kidderminster,
Worcs DY11 7RA
Tel: 01562 825252

A1 Security & Electrical Ltd
16 Brickfields
Huyton Trading Estate, Huyton
Merseyside L36 6HY
Tel: 0151 480 4455

Arjan SPRi (Mister Security)
Ave la Toison d'Or 25
1060 Brussels, Belgium
Tel: 02 511 0506

Ashley Security Products
PO Box No. 106
Willenhall
West Midlands WV12 5RQ
Tel: 01922 409533

Association of British Insurers
51 Gresham Street
London EC2V 7HQ
Tel: 0171 600 3333

Audioline Ltd (Moss Security)
2 Enfield Industrial Estate
Redditch, Worcs BN4 6BH
Tel: 01527 584584

Autolok Security Products Ltd
Park Lane, Royton
Oldham, Lancs OL2 6PU
Tel: 0161 624 8171

Automobile Inparts Ltd
7 Old Chapel Mews
Lake Street, Leighton Buzzard
Beds LU7 8RN
Tel: 01525 382713

Baddeley Rose Limited
Unit 9
Park Street Industrial Estate
Park Street, St Albans
Herts AL2 2DR
Tel: 01727 875301

Barrs Security
329 Fulham Palace Road
London SW6 6TE
Tel: 0171 736 7668

BC Technology, (Aiphone)
BC Tec House
Wallis Close
Park Farm South
Wellingborough
Northants NN8 6AG
Tel: 01933 405050

Benn Security
80 Wellingborough Road
Northampton NN1 4DP
Tel: 01604 20707

Beta-Thief Security Products Ltd
Unit K4-K5, Cherrycourt Way
Stanbridge Road
Leighton Buzzard
Beds LU7 8UH
Tel: 01525 853888

BodyGuard Security Ltd
Unit 10
Vermont Place, Tongwell
Milton Keynes MK15 8JA
Tel: 01908 218400

Bonwyke Group of Companies
Bonwyke House
41-43 Redlands Lane
Fareham, Hampshire PO14 1HL
Tel: 01329 289621

BPT Security Systems (UK) Ltd
Unit 16, Sovereign Park
Cleveland Way, Hemel Hempstead
Herts HP2 7DA
Tel: 01442 230800

British Standards Institution
2 Park Street
London W1A 2BS
Tel: 0171 629 9000

CeKa Abus
CeKa Works Ltd
Pwllheli, Gwynedd
North Wales LL53 5LH
Tel: 01758 701070

C & K Systems Ltd
Cunliffe Drive
Northfield Avenue, Kettering
Northamptonshire NN16 8LF
Tel: 01536 412202

Checkmate Devices
6 St Andrews Industrial Estate
Bridport, Dorset DT6 3EX
Tel: 01308 23871

Chubb Locks Ltd
PO Box 197
Wednesfield Road
Wolverhampton WV10 01ET
Tel: 01902 455440

Chubb Safe Equipment Co
PO Box 61
Wednesfield Road, Wolverhampton
West Midlands WV10 01EW
Tel: 01902 455111

Chubb Security Group
Chubb House
Staines Road West, Sunbury on Thames
Middlesex TW16 7AR
Tel: 01932 785588

Churchill Safes & Sec. Products
Brymbo Road Industrial Estate
Holditch, Newcastle-under-Lyme
Staffs ST5 9HZ
Tel: 01782 717400

Clifford Electronics Inc (UK)
Boundary Business Court
92/94 Church Road, Mitcham
Surrey CR4 3TD
Tel: 0181 646 8440

Crime Concern
Level 8
David Murray John Bldg
Brunel Centre, Swindon
Wiltshire SN1 1LY
Tel: 01793 514596

Dicon UK Ltd
19 St George's Road
Cheltenham
Gloucestershire GL50 3DT
Tel: 01242 222935

Dudley Safes
Unit 17
Deepdale Lane, Upper Gorral
Dudley, West Midlands DY3 2AF
Tel: 01384 239991

Electrical Contractors Association
ESCA House
34 Palace Court, Bayswater
London W2 4HY
Tel: 0171 229 1266

Eliza Tinsley & Co Ltd
Reddal Hill Road, Cradley Heath
West Midlands B64 5JF
Tel: 01384 66066

ERA Security Products
Straight Road
Short Heath, Willenhall
West Midlands WV12 5RA
Tel: 01922 710222

Euro Mul-T-Lock (UK) Ltd
Unit 4, Shieling Court
North Folds Road
Oakley Hay, Corby
Northamptonshire NN18 9QD
Tel: 01536 461111

Fire Protection Association
140 Aldersgate Street
London EC1A 4HX
Tel: 0171 600 1695

First Alert
4 The Paddock
Hambridge Road, Newbury
Berks RG14 5TQ
Tel: 01635 528100

FM Electronics Ltd
Forest Vale Road, Cinderford
Gloucestershire GL14 2PH
Tel: 01594 827070

Foxguard (Electronics) Ltd
Unit V, Wylds Road, Bridgwater
Somerset TA6 4BH
Tel: 01278 428473

Glass and Glazing Federation
44-48 Borough High Street
London SE1 1XB
Tel: 0171 403 7177

Guardall *(see Chubb Security)*

Hamber Safes
Radford Way, Billericay
Essex CM12 01EG
Tel: 01277 624450

Homeguard Products
Unit 1
Hyle Farm, Sherborne
Dorset DT9 6EE
Tel: 01935 815576

Ingersoll *(see Yale Security Products)*

Jacksons Fine Fencing
337 Stowting Common
Nr Ashford
Kent TN25 6BN
Tel: 01233 750393

Laminated Glass Information Centre
299 Oxford Street
London W1R 1LA
Tel: 0171 499 1720

LCB Marketing
Greenacres International Group
Old Dartford Road, Farningham
Kent DA4 01EB
Tel: 01322 866313

Lionweld Kennedy Ltd
Marsh Road, Middlesbrough
Cleveland TS1 5JS
Tel: 01642 245151

Locksecure Services Ltd
5 London Road, Sevenoaks
Kent TN13 1AH
Tel: 01732 459908

Markitwise International
Homme Castle Farm, Shelsley Walsh
Worcestershire WR6 6RR
Tel: 01886 812427

Master Locksmiths Association
Unit 4/5, Business Park
Great Central Way
Woodford Halse, Daventry
Northamptonshire NN11 6PZ
Tel: 01327 62255

Menvier Security Ltd
Hither Green, Clevedon
Avon BS21 6XU
Tel: 01272 870078

Metro Products Ltd
98-102 Station Road East, Oxted
Surrey RH8 01AY
Tel: 01883 717644

Moat Doors
(Status Electronics Ltd)
Link House
42 Chigwell Lane, Loughton
Essex 1G10 3NZ
Tel: 0181 502 0136

Moorhouse Marketing
(Siemens Light)
Moorlynch, Bridgwater
Somerset TA7 9BT
Tel: 01458 210569

National Caravan Council
Catherine House
Victoria Road, Aldershot
Hants GU11 1SS
Tel: 01252 318251

National Approval Council
for Security Systems (NACOSS)
Queensgate House
14 Cookham Road, Maidenhead
Berkshire SL6 8AJ
Tel: 01628 37512

National House Building Council
(NHBC)
Buildmark House
Chiltern Avenue, Amersham
Bucks HP6 5AP
Tel: 01494 434477

Paxton Automation Ltd
Unit 1, Shepherd Industrial Estate
Brooks Road, Lewes
East Sussex BN7 2BY
Tel: 01273 474509

Personal Watercraft Association
(PWA)
Woodside House
Woodside Road, Eastleigh
Hampshire SO5 4ET
Tel: 01703 616888

Pilkington Glass Consultants
Prescot Road
St Helens WA10 3TT
Tel: 01744 692000

Response Electronics PLC
Unit 1, First Quarter
Longmead Industrial Estate
Epsom, Surrey KT19 9QN
Tel: 01372 744330

Retainacar Limited
45 Tonsley Place
London SW18 1BH
Tel: 0181 871 1333

The Royal Society for the Prevention
of Accidents (RoSPA)
Cannon House
The Priory, Queensway
Birmingham B4 6BS
Tel: 0121 200 2461

Safe & Secure Ltd
3 Swanscombe Road
Holland Park
London W11 4SU
Tel: 0171 371 2242

Safeways Security Products Ltd
10 Grange Mount
Birkenhead L43 4XW
Tel: 0151 653 3414

Scantronic Ltd
Perivale Industrial Park, Greenford
Middlesex UB6 7RJ
Tel: 0181 991 1133

Securikey Ltd
PO Box 18, Aldershot
Hants GU12 4SL
Tel: 01252 311888

Security Services Association
70-71 Camden Street, North Shields
Tyne & Wear NE30 1NH
Tel: 0191 296 3242

Security Window Shutters
Unit 2, Middlegate White Lund Industrial
Estate, Morecambe
Lancs LA3 3BN
Tel: 01524 33986

Selmar Alarms
The Causeway, Malden
Essex CM9 7LW
Tel: 01621 854488

Sentry Safes
6 The Business Village
Pebble Close, Tamworth
Staffs B77 4RD
Tel: 01827 311888

Simba Security Systems
Security House
Occupation Road
London SE17 3BE
Tel: 0171 703 0485

Smiths Industries Environmental
Controls Co Ltd, Apsley Way
London NW2 7UR
Tel: 0181 450 8944

Solartrack PLC
42 New Road, Dagenham
Essex RM9 6YS
Tel: 0181 595 1218

Sparkrite
Stadium Consumer Products Division
Stephen House
Brenda Road, Hartlepool
Cleveland TS25 2BQ
Tel: 01429 862616

Superswitch Electric Appliances Ltd
Houldsworth Street
Reddish, Stockport
Cheshire SK5 6BZ
Tel: 0161 431 4885

TrakBak
Securicor Datatrak
Securicor Alarms
Auckland House
New Zealand Avenue
Walton-on-Thames
Surrey KT12 1PL
Tel: 01932 252222

Tunstall Telecom Ltd
Whitley Lodge, Whitley Bridge
Yorkshire DN14 01HR
Tel: 01977 661234

UK ID Systems
Riverside Industrial Park
Catterall
Preston PR3 01HP
Tel: 01995 606451

Viper Security Ltd
Lynch Lane, Weymouth
Dorset DT4 9DG
Tel: 01305 783801

Yale Security Products
(& Ingersoll)
Wood Street, Willenhall
West Midlands WV13 1LA
Tel: 01902 366911

Index

A

B

C

D

E

Acknowledgements

Written by	Sonia Aarons
	Donna Gilbert
Editor	Derek Jones
Design	Dave Hermelin
	Rhian Walters
Indexed	Rachel Rogers

The authors would like to express their thanks to the following for their help in compiling this book:

Advanced Design Electronics
Association of British Insurers
Benn Security of Northampton
BPT Systems
Chubb Security Group
Codalarm
David Darby (for his endless patience in photographing the fitting sequences).
Lynn East
ERA Security Products
Stuart Mundy of Hackney DIY
Hamber Safes
George Hodge
Dave Kennard
John Little Associates
Rachel Witts of The Laminated Glass Information Centre
Ken Marsden of Locksecure Services, Sevenoaks (for his assistance and advice in carrying out the lock fitting sequences)
John Gosling of Prolec Services (for his assistance and advice in carrying out our alarm fitting sequence)
Security Publications
Smiths Industries
Sgt Peter Hardy, Sussex Police
Martyn Williams (for his assistance and advice in carrying out the car alarm fitting sequence)